# Praise for *Thinking about Thinking*

"Dr. Carol Benton has provided an excellent resource for music teachers. I recommend it for both the theoretical research and the practical applications offered. *Thinking about Thinking* should be essential reading for ALL teachers and musicians."—**Frank E. Folds**, director of bands, Alton C. Crews Middle School; president, Georgia Music Educators Association

"Accessible to music researchers and music teachers alike, Benton's work is situated at the intersection of cognitive theory and applied practice. Using concrete examples, each chapter provides a theoretical and empirical overview of metacognition as it exists in musical contexts, yet never strays from the practical application to music instruction. This synthesis of research on metacognition in music serves as a timely contribution to the field."—**Meghan Bathgate**, MA, research psychology PhD candidate, cognitive psychology, University of Pittsburgh

"Dr. Carol Benton reminds us that the goal of music teaching (or any teaching) is more than a successful performance. Our goal is to fully understand why the student's effort was successful or not. Our pedagogy, after all, is driven by this deeper understanding of internal processes. The metacognitive strategies presented in her book provide the reflective music teacher with a repertoire of tools through which the teacher can reveal the student's true understanding and mastery of the task at hand. As such, her work contributes to both the practice of music teaching and the training of future successful music teachers."—**Richard Kennel**, dean and professor of performance studies at the College of Musical Arts, Bowling Green State University

# THINKING ABOUT THINKING

## Metacognition for Music Learning

**Carol W. Benton**

PUBLISHED IN PARTNERSHIP WITH NAfME:
NATIONAL ASSOCIATION FOR MUSIC EDUCATION

ROWMAN & LITTLEFIELD EDUCATION

A division of
ROWMAN & LITTLEFIELD
Lanham • Boulder • New York • Toronto • Plymouth, UK

Published in partnership with NAfME: National Association for Music Education

Published by Rowman & Littlefield Education
A division of Rowman & Littlefield
4501 Forbes Boulevard, Suite 200, Lanham, Maryland 20706
www.rowman.com

10 Thornbury Road, Plymouth PL6 7PP, United Kingdom

British Library Cataloguing in Publication Information Available

**Library of Congress Cataloging-in-Publication Data**
Benton, Carol, 1950- author.
  Thinking about thinking : metacognition for music learning / Carol Benton.
    pages cm
  Includes bibliographical references.
  ISBN 978-1-4758-0511-6 (cloth : alk. paper) — ISBN 978-1-4758-0512-3 (pbk. : alk. paper) — ISBN 978-1-4758-0513-0 (electronic) 1. Music—Instruction and study. 2. Metacognition. I. Title.
  MT1.B525 2014
  780.71—dc23

                                                            2013044426

∞™ The paper used in this publication meets the minimum requirements of American National Standard for Information Sciences—Permanence of Paper for Printed Library Materials, ANSI/NISO Z39.48-1992.

Printed in the United States of America

# CONTENTS

# ILLUSTRATIONS

## PHOTOGRAPHS

All photos courtesy of the author.

# FIGURES

# TABLE

# FOREWORD

In her book *Thinking about Thinking: Metacognition for Music Learning*, Dr. Carol W. Benton has provided a well-researched approach to the teaching and learning of music through metacognitive instructional strategies. She introduces the book through a well-defined chapter on metacognition with an attendant discussion on its forty-year history. Dr. Benton has presented an informative overview in her purpose statement by telling her readers that the book on metacognition in music is not limited to any one type of music teaching. She makes reference to general-music teachers (at all levels), middle and high school band and orchestra directors, choral directors, and applied-music studio teachers. Throughout each chapter, Dr. Benton recommends ways in which music teachers can incorporate metacognitive instructional strategies into their teaching. She discusses the different levels of student music ability from novice to advanced in which teachers may find ways to use metacognition to assist students in becoming better musicians. According to Dr. Benton, the use of megacognition also promotes the avoidance of boredom and frustration that often leads to attrition in music-education programs.

While Dr. Benton's book is about the use of metacognition in working with music students, she has not forgotten the importance of the role of megacognition in the life of the teacher. She discusses the importance of thinking about thinking (metacognition) as each teacher prepares assignments, procedures, activities, and behaviors that require students to think about thinking in content instruction, rehearsals, creative projects, and independent practice.

With both students and teachers involved in metacognition on a daily basis, Dr. Benton has provided an exceptional model for both students and teachers to become independent, lifelong music learners. It is with pleasure that I recommend this excellent book to music educators regardless of their assignment or teaching level.

Irma H. Collins, DMA
Founder, *Journal of Music Teacher Education*

# PREFACE

I enjoyed my years as a chorus teacher in middle and high schools. Many students participated in my ensembles, with varying degrees of talent and enthusiasm. I felt good about giving them opportunities to not only participate in choral singing but also develop a sense of themselves as people who could make a contribution to the world around them through music. Together, my students and I worked toward musical excellence, and I was conscious of teaching content standards in a comprehensive manner so that my students could acquire musical understanding as well as performance skill.

As the years went by, I had a nagging concern that I needed to find ways to help some of my students become engaged in a more mindful way during chorus classes and rehearsals. I always had a few students who, although demonstrating natural music ability (such as accurate intonation or sensitivity to rhythm), appeared to participate in a rote manner, without thinking about what they were doing. Yes, these students did eventually learn their parts and perform successfully in the concerts, but it seemed that rote repetition was the method by which they learned just enough to get by. Therefore, I continued to have the feeling that there must be some way to promote deeper and more thoughtful learning among this group of students who appeared to participate in a relatively mindless way.

Then I discovered some research reports on the topic of *metacognition*, most simply defined as *thinking about thinking*. Moreover, I discovered some instructional strategies and classroom activities that I could implement to promote metacognition among students, and I began to incorporate these activities into my chorus classes. It was not a magic potion. My students did not immediately sing with perfect blend, balance, and diction because I was requiring them to engage in metacognitive activities. But I did see them become more musically self-aware, more musically independent, and more interested in their own progress as young musicians.

I considered the metacognitive activities as tools for teaching musicianship, and I do not recall that I ever used the word *metacognition* while teaching my students. Nevertheless, the infusion of metacognitive strategies somehow created a subtle change in the classroom environment, resulting in elevating the typical dialogue of daily rehearsals. Specifically, I asked my students to participate in three metacognitive activities on a somewhat regular basis over the course of each school year: (1) self-reflective writing in response to prompts that I provided, (2) self-assessment activities where students identified their strengths and weaknesses and evaluated their own musical progress, and (3) think-aloud sessions where students shared learning strategies with partners as they worked on sight-singing or music theory assignments.

*Metacognition* is a term that has been defined in various ways by various researchers. Perhaps it is best to think of it as an umbrella term that covers an array of thinking and learning strategies. My personal conclusion is that metacognition is a pervasive mindset that can enrich teaching and learning. Armed with some knowledge about metacognition, a teacher can create a classroom environment where students are encouraged to plan, monitor, and evaluate their own learning, using reflection and strategizing as tools for success.

In this book, I hope that readers will find some helpful ideas to enrich their teaching, especially with regard to facilitating development of metacognitive skills among students in music classes.

# ACKNOWLEDGMENTS

I would like to express my thanks to several colleagues and friends for their help in preparing this book for publication. Thanks to Beth Childress, Heather Moore, and Dr. Grace Ohlenbusch for providing feedback and suggestions. Thanks to excellent music educators Ray Ellis, Sean McBride, and Leah Nestor for allowing me into their music classrooms. Thanks to Dr. Irma Collins for her interest and support. Finally, thanks to my husband, Charlie, for his interest and support throughout the writing process.

# ❶

# THINKING ABOUT THINKING: WHAT IS METACOGNITION?

The simplest way to define *metacognition* is to say that it consists of thinking about thinking. Used by learners to acquire knowledge, understanding, and skill for accomplishing educational objectives, metacognition is a transcendent and executive type of thinking that can positively affect learning outcomes. When learners use metacognition, they become aware of their own thought processes, plan and monitor their own learning, assess their own progress, and evaluate the products of their efforts. These actions result in development of progressively greater degrees of self-awareness and self-regulation. It follows, then, that practicing metacognition leads to learner independence and lifelong learning. In this chapter, several definitions of metacognition are presented along with a historical overview of some of the research on the topic.

A dictionary definition of *cognition* tells us that it is "the act or process of knowing in the broadest sense" and "an intellectual process by which knowledge is gained about perceptions or ideas."[1] Thus, when a learner uses *metacognition*, the object of the learner's thinking is the personal act of knowing or the intellectual process of gaining knowledge. Metacognition, this circular idea of thinking about thinking, is best understood as an overarching construct that encompasses numerous habits and actions used by learners. Researchers and writers define metacognition in various ways, so a universal definition is hard to pin down. Nevertheless, an abundance of research exists to suggest that music educators might want to apply some instructional strategies that have been shown to help students develop metacognitive skills. These skills become tools for acquiring content knowledge about music, developing performance skills, or improvising and composing music.[2]

Moreover, metacognition may be practiced for acquisition of knowledge and skill in any academic discipline. Because the metacognitive learner develops self-awareness and control of personal thought processes, it is a type of thinking that transcends learning domains and is not limited to any one academic subject area.[3] In fact, much of the research on metacognition has been carried out in areas such as reading and math education. For this reason, it is helpful to begin this book with an exploration of research from the general-education arena to gain a better understanding of what metacognition is. This can be done with assurance that productive metacognitive skills for reading, math, science, problem solving, and decision making can be adapted by informed music educators and applied to music teaching and learning.

## A BRIEF HISTORY OF THE RESEARCH ON METACOGNITION

The term *metacognition* has been in the vocabulary of educators for almost forty years. John Flavell brought groundbreaking research to the education community in the 1970s through his writings about *metamemory* and *metacognition*. "Metacognition," according to Flavell,

> refers to one's own knowledge concerning one's own cognitive processes and products or anything related to them (e.g., the learning-relevant properties of information or data). For example, I am engaging in metacognition (metamemory, metalearning, metaattention, metalanguage, or whatever) if I notice that I am having more trouble learning A than B, if it strikes me that I should double-check C before accepting it as a fact, if it occurs to me that I had better scrutinize each and every alternative in any multiple-choice-type task situation before deciding which is the best one, if I become aware that I am not sure what the experimenter really wants me to do, if I sense that I had better make a note of D because I may

forget it, if I think to ask someone about E to see if I have it right. Such examples could be multiplied endlessly. In any kind of cognitive transaction with the human or nonhuman environment, a variety of information-processing activities may go on. Metacognition refers, among other things, to the active monitoring and consequent regulation and orchestration of these processes in relation to the cognitive objects or data on which they bear, usually in the service of some concrete goal or objective.[4]

The idea of identifying and promoting this type of thinking resonated with educators. For many, it was an attractive premise that metacognition helps learners to gain knowledge and skill. Following Flavell's initial research, other educational researchers put forth their own definitions and analyses of metacognition. Three examples are offered here.

1. In 1984, Arthur Costa defined metacognition as "our ability to know what we know and what we don't know. It occurs in the cerebral cortex and is thought by some neurologists to be uniquely human. Metacognition is our ability to plan a strategy for producing what information is needed, to be conscious of our own steps and strategies during the act of problem solving, and to reflect on and evaluate the productivity of our own thinking."[5]
2. In 1991, John Barell offered the following on metacognition. "Usually," he said, "we consider metacognition in terms of our awareness of how we think about a certain task or problem. . . . So metacognition focuses upon the mental processes we use within a specific situation. . . . Another aspect of metacognitive awareness and control is not always mentioned: knowledge of, awareness of, and control of the feelings that accompany certain situations."[6]
3. In 2006, Michael Martinez said that "metacognition is the monitoring and control of thought. . . . The toolbox is an equally apt metaphor for metacognition."[7]

## Metacognition and the Thinking-Skills Movement

Metacognition involves thinking skills that are sometimes classified as being of a *higher order*. Since the 1980s, educators have been aware of the need to teach thinking skills that are labeled as *critical, creative*, and *higher order*. Teachers who emphasize higher-order thinking skills know that simply covering content does not ensure that students will learn to think effectively and independently. In 1986, Presseisen defined metacognition in light of the thinking-skills movement, stating that it encompasses "the learning to learn skills aimed at making thinking more conscious and the student more aware of the ways one can go about problem solving or decision making."[8] She went on to suggest that "perhaps the most striking aspect of teaching thinking in the current movement is the emphasis on metacognitive ways of thinking."[9]

In 1998 Halpern proposed metacognition as one component of a four-part model for teaching critical thinking, stating that metacognitive monitoring of thought processes enables the learner to guide the use of critical-thinking skills. Specifically, Halpern emphasized the importance of metacognitive actions such as goal setting, checking for accuracy, and monitoring the expenditure of time and mental energy in pursuit of a learning goal.[10] Kuhn, another researcher who places metacognition in the realm of critical-thinking skills, proposed that metacognition is implicit in all models of critical thinking as a second-order thinking skill that builds on first-order declarative knowledge and allows the learner to exert control over thought processes. According to Kuhn, central metacognitive questions for any learner are, "What do I know, and how do I know it?"[11]

## METACOGNITION: CONTENT SPECIFIC AND DISCIPLINE TRANSCENDENT

Learners do not practice metacognition in isolation from the content of their studies. It is not like weight lifting as an isolated activity that helps football players to prepare for the game. Instead, metacognition is a type of thinking that helps students while they are engaged in learning tasks that are directly embedded in a specific discipline. For this reason we say that metacognition is content specific.

Richard Colwell asserted that critical thinking is inextricably linked with content knowledge in a specific domain or discipline. He explained that "what we do know about thinking is that it is subject matter–specific. Scholars think in a discipline: one thinks like a historian or like a musician. The process of thinking is intertwined with the content of thought—domain knowledge."[12] Similarly, Chiu and Kuo stated that basic metacognitive training begins with domain-specific language and tasks. According to them, metacognitive training within a discipline helps students to recognize prior knowledge, learn how to find new information, assimilate new learning with prior knowledge, and recognize errors that are common to the discipline.[13]

Let us consider an example of learners using metacognition within the music discipline. Music students learn how to count rhythm patterns within specific meters. With practice, they develop the ability to monitor their rhythmic accuracy, recognize rhythm mistakes, and apply strategies to correct those mistakes. Knowledge of the time values of notes within the contexts of various meters is classified as declarative knowledge or content knowledge within the music discipline and, therefore, requires cognition. But when music learners become aware that they have made rhythm mistakes—and they take action to make corrections—they are applying metacognition. Specifically, the learners are using the metacognitive skills of self-awareness, self-monitoring, and strategy use to accomplish the goal of rhythmic accuracy. Music learners are thinking like musicians when they apply metacognition to achieve musical goals.

Although metacognition is applied in discipline-specific learning situations, it does possess a transcendent, executive quality. It is the type of thinking whereby learners guide their intellectual efforts in any content area; and it is, therefore, domain general.[14] Gagné and Driscoll identified several executive (metacognitive) strategies of critical thinking, including "goal-setting, concentration, management, and self-monitoring."[15] Halpern stated that metacognition is the "boss" function that enables learners to plan, monitor, and carry out cognitive actions.[16] Brown labeled metacognition as the "central processor" or "overseer" of learners' thoughts.[17]

In a 2001 revision of Bloom's taxonomy of educational objectives, Anderson et al. included metacognition as one of four major types of knowledge in the "knowledge dimension" of the taxonomy. Defining metacognitive knowledge as "knowledge of cognition in general as well as awareness and knowledge of one's own cognition," taxonomy revisionists asserted that metacognition includes "strategic knowledge; knowledge about cognitive tasks, including appropriate contextual and conditional knowledge; and self-knowledge."[18] As such, metacognition takes its place as an important component of the twenty-first-century version of Bloom's taxonomy. Regarding their choice to include metacognition in the revised taxonomy, the authors stated that "our inclusion of *metacognitive knowledge* is predicated on our belief that it is extremely important in understanding and facilitating learning, a belief that is consistent with the basic precepts of cognitive psychology and supported by empirical research."[19]

## METACOGNITION AND CHILD DEVELOPMENT

A review of the literature yields conflicting opinions regarding when children develop the ability to engage in metacognitive thought. Some researchers suggest that metacognition begins in early childhood, while others assert that it is not until adolescence that children become capable of metacognition. Researchers generally agree that adolescents in middle school and high school years are thoroughly able to exercise metacognitive skills. Some researchers point to early childhood experiences that lay the foundation for metacognitive skill building.

For example, Dawson and Guare stated that the roots of metacognition are seen in infancy when children first begin to sort and classify objects and when they first begin to perceive cause-effect relationships. Further, they asserted that when toddlers and young children learn to observe daily rituals and routines, they are beginning to use metacognition.[20] On the other hand, Kuhn suggested that the foundation of metacognitive thinking is laid somewhere around ages three to five and that metacognition does not fully develop until adolescence.[21] Waters and Kunnmann found that first graders could engage in metacognition when trained and prompted by their teachers and that first graders were able to transfer metacognitive skills from one context to another as they moved from first to second grade.[22]

It is apparent that researchers have different opinions regarding precise developmental patterns for metacognition. In general, it appears safe to say that teachers may guide children in primary grades to begin building basic metacognitive skills and that teachers might expect students from upper elementary grades through high school and college to use metacognition in increasingly independent ways.

## COMPONENTS OF METACOGNITION

In a review of the literature, several components of metacognition emerge as recurrent themes, summarized in the list below. When a learner practices metacognition,

- The learner is increasingly self-aware.
- The learner exerts control over personal thought processes.
- The learner engages in self-regulation.
- The learner becomes increasingly independent in learning tasks.
- The learner selects and applies learning strategies.
- The learner monitors personal progress through a learning task.
- The learner modifies learning strategies and seeks resources or assistance when needed.
- The learner reflects on learning.
- The learner engages in self-evaluation (self-assessment).

**Photo 1.1.   Elementary Choir and Ensemble**

## METACOGNITIVE SKILLS

Metacognition involves the monitoring and control of thought processes.[23] As such, it requires heightened self-awareness and development of metacognitive thinking skills. Researchers delineate metacognitive skills in three broad categories that encompass (1) planning for a learning task, (2) monitoring thought processes during a learning task, and (3) evaluating the product(s) of a completed learning task.[24] Marzano and Kendall use different terminology when they observe that the "metacognitive system has four functions: (1) specifying goals, (2) process monitoring, (3) monitoring clarity, and (4) monitoring accuracy."[25]

Despite slight differences in wording, it is apparent that researchers see metacognitive skills as specific activities requiring learners to demonstrate mindfulness in a sequential manner throughout a learning task. Moreover, researchers agree that learners should engage in planning and goal setting in beginning stages of a learning task with self-monitoring applied to ongoing activities through the progression of a learning task. When learners engage in metacognition, they develop the ability to distinguish between what they know and what they do not know. This important skill is labeled *knowledge monitoring*. Researchers have found a positive correlation between learners' knowledge-monitoring ability and their scholastic aptitude. Learners who exhibit the ability to monitor their learning also exhibit higher levels of scholastic achievement.[26]

### Planning for Learning: A Metacognitive Skill

Metacognitive learners define their learning tasks, decide what they are supposed to do, and gain an understanding from the teacher of what a successful outcome will be. These learners then set personal goals and select strategies for accomplishing their goals. In this process, the learners consider their available resources of time, materials, equipment, and previous knowledge and skill.

Let us consider a scenario depicting a fourth grade general-music student who is assigned to work with a partner to create a two-measure rhythmic ostinato in 4/4 meter. He gains an understanding from his teacher that he and his partner may choose their rhythm instruments and that they have ten minutes to complete the task before performing their ostinato as accompaniment to a rhythmic chant performed by other students. As the learner checks his understanding of the task, he asks his teacher about specific parameters, such as how many beats he and his partner should have in their ostinato pattern. He assesses his own prior knowledge of ostinati and rhythm patterns in 4/4 meter, as well as his partner's knowledge about the task. They remember that they have played patterns in music class on previous occasions. Together, the learner and his partner select two wood blocks and set about the task. They decide that each boy will create a one-measure rhythm pattern and that they will put their patterns together for a two-measure ostinato.

## Monitoring Learning: A Metacognitive Skill

Metacognitive learners engage in self-assessment throughout learning tasks. They pose internal questions such as "How am I doing?" "Do I think I am on the right track?" "Have I completed the necessary steps for this assignment?" The learners compare their ongoing products of learning with preconceived models or standards of excellence and accuracy. If they run into obstacles, metacognitive learners revise their strategies. Monitoring learning requires learners to keep their original goals in mind and to continually check their progress toward achievement of those goals.

Returning to our scenario—the fourth-grade general-music student begins to experiment with sounds on the wood block that he selected for his task. He improvises several rhythm patterns and decides which pattern he likes best. As he listens, he checks to see whether he can count four beats in his rhythmic pattern. He realizes that he probably has too many beats in his pattern, so he revises it to more closely approximate the original goal of creating one measure of an ostinato in 4/4 meter. Satisfied that he has created a one-measure rhythm pattern in 4/4 meter, the student turns to his partner and suggests that they put their patterns together for the two-measure finished product. He suggests that his partner play the first measure, allowing him to add his pattern for the second measure. Their first attempts are rhythmically unsteady; but after several practice runs the partners decide that they have a steady and rhythmically interesting two-measure ostinato pattern in 4/4 meter.

## Evaluating Learning: A Metacognitive Skill

Metacognitive learners engage in self-evaluation of a summative nature at the completion of learning tasks. They pose internal questions such as "How did I do?" "Was my finished product successful?" "Could I have done something differently or better?" "How can I use this new learning in the future?" This step allows learners to plan for future learning. Will they need to revisit current tasks to achieve success? Or are they ready to go on to more challenging tasks? As they evaluate the products of their efforts and plan for future learning, the learners begin the metacognition cycle anew.

In the final stage of our scenario—the fourth-grade general-music student and his partner play their two-measure ostinato pattern repetitively while a group of their classmates performs a rhythmic chant. They are able to maintain a steady beat, and their rhythm pattern is interesting and complimentary to the chant. As the teacher congratulates the group on their performance, the learner and his partner decide that they are pleased with the outcome of their efforts. The learner concludes that he understands 4/4 meter and that he is competent in creating a rhythmic ostinato. He looks forward to future opportunities to engage in creative-music activities. He and his partner decide that during their next music class they will expand their ostinato and invite two friends to join them on hand drums.

---

### Tips for Teachers

At the beginning of a music class or rehearsal, ask each student to write a personal, musical goal for the day on a 3" × 5" notecard. At the end of the class or rehearsal, ask students to add brief evaluations of whether they achieved their goals. Collect and read the cards to glimpse your students' goal-setting and self-assessment abilities.

## THREE TYPES OF METACOGNITIVE KNOWLEDGE

In much the same way that researchers define three distinct metacognitive skills (planning, self-monitoring, and self-evaluation), Schraw delineates three types of metacognitive knowledge. Learners use *declarative*, *procedural*, and *conditional* metacognitive knowledge as they work through learning tasks.[27] The teacher who endeavors to help students use metacognition for positive learning outcomes will encourage them to build knowledge in these three areas.

1. Declarative knowledge is knowledge *about* something. When learners know about themselves as learners (their strengths, weaknesses, and preferences), they possesses declarative metacognitive knowledge about themselves.
2. Procedural knowledge is knowledge about *how to do* something. When learners devise and apply personal learning strategies that help them to succeed in learning situations, they are developing procedural metacognitive knowledge.
3. Conditional knowledge refers to knowing *when and why* (under what circumstances) to apply strategies. When learners apply appropriate strategies in a timely fashion to achieve positive learning outcomes, they are using conditional metacognitive knowledge.[28]

All three types of knowledge are components of metacognition. It is important to note that the three types of metacognitive knowledge are personal and unique for each learner and might vary from one learning situation to another. Ideally, learners apply declarative, procedural, and conditional types of metacognitive knowledge that pertain to specific learning situations and that help them to achieve positive learning outcomes.

## TEACHABLE SKILLS

John Dewey, eminent educational philosopher of the early twentieth century, asserted that "learning is learning to think."[29] At a glance, the list of skills and components of metacognition appears to be a commonsense list of thinking habits used by excellent students in any educational setting. Educators recognize that good students engage in these behaviors on a regular basis. At the same time, educators also recognize that not all students use metacognitive skills naturally or routinely. Many students learn by rote, expecting their teachers to spoon-feed information to them every step along the way. Although physically present in a classroom, these students do not cognitively engage in learning tasks in an active and independent way. This phenomenon can occur in music classes as well as in academic classes. Pogonowski observed that "it is possible for students to sit through years of general-music classes and never be asked to reflect upon a musical problem. . . . It is possible for students to sit through an entire rehearsal and only be aware of their own parts. In a performance setting in general-music class, or in chorus, orchestra, and band rehearsals, students can learn to think more effectively about and beyond their particular parts."[30]

The good news is that metacognitive skills can be taught.[31] Educators have devised many effective teaching strategies and classroom activities that promote metacognition among learners. For example, to help young children develop the executive skills of planning and prioritizing, teachers can break down large assignments into smaller, sequential steps. By the time students reach middle school, they will be expected to function in this way independently.[32]

## Caution Regarding Overemphasis on Metacognition

Having extolled the virtues of metacognition, it is wise to insert a caveat regarding its overemphasis in teaching and learning. For example, in music education, the acts of listening to, creating, and performing music remain at the core of the curriculum. Metacognitive skills may serve as tools for students as they pursue music-learning objectives; however, metacognition is not the end product of instruction. In *The Schools We Need and Why We Don't Have Them*, Hirsch admonished educators regarding an overemphasis on metacognition, especially if it is taught as an abstract concept outside of domain-specific content learning.[33] He asserted that an overemphasis on metacognition can overload learners' working memories and interfere with development of problem-solving capacity and procedural competency. Moreover,

Hirsch stated that these negative effects might be most apparent among disadvantaged children and slow learners.[34]

It is prudent, therefore, for teachers to consider an emphasis on metacognition to be a complement to regular music instruction. As music educators plan and deliver instruction on a daily basis, they can incorporate teaching strategies and classroom activities that require students to use metacognitive skills. Teachers might find that metacognitive skills facilitate music learning and help students develop independence.

## THE PURPOSE OF THIS BOOK

While investigating metacognition as a transcendent, domain-general, and beneficial habit for learners in all disciplines, this book will focus primarily on the usefulness of metacognition in music learning. Throughout the book, we will explore research on metacognition in music education and see how metacognitive instructional strategies might be applied in music-teaching and -learning scenarios. For this reason, the contents of this book are not limited to any one type of music teaching. General-music teachers, middle and high school band and orchestra directors, choral directors, and applied-music studio teachers will find ideas that might be applied to their particular teaching circumstances. The purpose of the book is to present information acquired through research along with practical suggestions for music educators who want to elevate the level of cognitive engagement among their students by promoting metacognition. The overarching goal is to provide students with cognitive tools to become independent, lifelong music learners.

## NOTES

1. *Webster's Third New International Dictionary*, s.v. "cognition," (Springfield, MA: Merriam-Webster, Inc. 1986), 440.

2. Lenore Pogonowski, "Metacognition: A Dimension of Musical Thinking," in *Dimensions of Musical Thinking*, edited by Eunice Boardman (Reston, Va.: MENC, 1989), 9–19.

3. Ann Brown, "Knowing When, Where, and How to Remember: A Problem of Metacognition," in *Advances in Instructional Psychology, volume 1,* edited by Robert Glaser (Hillsdale, N.J.: Lawrence Erlbaum Associates, 1978), 80; Michael A. Peters, "Kinds of Thinking, Styles of Reasoning," in *Critical Thinking and Learning,* edited by Mark Mason (Malden, Mass.: Blackwell Publishing, 2008), 13; Shawn Taylor, "Better Learning through Better Thinking: Developing Students' Metacognitive Abilities," *Journal of College Reading and Learning* 30, no. 1 (1999): 42; Howard T. Everson, Sigmund Tobias, and Vytas Laitusis, "Do Metacognitive Skills and Learning Strategies Transfer across Domains?" (paper presented at the Annual Meeting of the American Educational Research Association, Chicago, Ill., March 24–28, 1997), 11.

4. John H. Flavell, "Metacognitive Aspects of Problem Solving," in *The Nature of Intelligence,* edited by Lauren B. Resnick (Hillsdale, N.J.: Lawrence Erlbaum Associates, 1976), 232.

5. Arthur L. Costa, "Mediating the Metacognitive," *Educational Leadership* 42 (1984): 57.

6. John Barell, *Teaching for Thoughtfulness: Classroom Strategies to Enhance Intellectual Development* (White Plains, N.Y.: Longman Publishing Group, 1991), 207.

7. Michael E. Martinez, "What Is Metacognition?" *Phi Delta Kappan* 87, no. 9 (2006): 696.

8. Barbara Z. Presseisen, *Thinking Skills: Research and Practice* (Washington, D.C.: National Education Association, 1986), 9.

9. Ibid., 12.

10. Diane F. Halpern, "Teaching Critical Thinking for Transfer across Domains: Dispositions, Skills, Structure Training, and Metacognitive Monitoring," *American Psychologist* 53, no. 4 (1998): 454.

11. Deanna Kuhn, "A Developmental Model of Critical Thinking," *Educational Researcher* 28, no. 2 (1999): 17.

12. Richard Colwell, "Roles of Direct Instruction, Critical Thinking, and Transfer in the Design of Curriculum for Music Learning," in *MENC Handbook of Research on Music Learning: vol. 1, Strategies,* edited by Richard Colwell and Peter R. Webster (New York: Oxford University Press, 2011), 108.

13. Ming Ming Chiu and Sze Wing Kuo, "Social Metacognition in Groups: Benefits, Difficulties, Learning, and Teaching," in *Metacognition: New Research Developments,* edited by Clayton B. Larson (New York: Nova Science Publishers, 2009), 129.

14. Gregory Schraw, "Promoting General Metacognitive Awareness," in *Metacognition in Learning and Instruction: Theory, Research and Practice,*

edited by Hope Hartman (Dordrecht, Netherlands: Kluwer Academic Publishers, 2001), 5.

15. Robert M. Gagné and Mary Perkins Driscoll, *Essentials of Learning for Instruction* (Englewood Cliffs, N.J.: Prentice-Hall, 1988), 96.

16. Halpern, "Teaching Critical Thinking," 454.

17. Brown, "Knowing When, Where, and How," 81.

18. Lorin W. Anderson, David R. Krathwohl, Peter W. Airasian, Kathleen A. Cruikshank, Richard E. Mayer, Paul R. Pintrich, James Raths, and Merlin C. Wittrock, *A Taxonomy for Learning, Teaching, and Assessing: A Revision of Bloom's Taxonomy of Education Objectives* (New York: Longman, 2001), 29.

19. Ibid., 44.

20. Peg Dawson and Richard Guare, *Smart but Scattered: The Revolutionary "Executive Skills" Approach to Helping Kids Reach Their Potential* (New York: Guilford Press, 2009), 273.

21. Kuhn, "A Developmental Model," 19.

22. Harriet S. Waters and Thomas W. Kunnmann, "Metacognition and Strategy Discovery in Early Childhood," in *Metacognition, Strategy Use, and Instruction*, edited by Harriet S. Waters and Wolfgang Schneider (New York: Guilford Press, 2009), 20.

23. Martinez, "What is Metacognition?" 696.

24. Barell, *Teaching for Thoughtfulness*, 209; Barry K. Beyer, *Practical Strategies for the Teaching of Thinking* (Boston: Allyn and Bacon, 1987), 173; John Dunlosky and Janet Metcalfe, *Metacognition* (Thousand Oaks, Calif.: SAGE Publications, 2009), 202–204; Pat Goldberg, *Increasing Problem Solving through the Metacognitive Skills of Planning, Monitoring, and Evaluating*, Eric Document ED 439 160 (Chicago: Spencer Foundation, 1999), 6–8.

25. Robert J. Marzano and John S. Kendall, *Designing and Assessing Education Objectives: Applying the New Taxonomy* (Thousand Oaks, Calif.: Corwin Press, 2008), 21.

26. Sigmund, Tobias, Howard T. Everson, and Vytas Laitusis, "Towards a Performance Based Measure of Metacognitive Knowledge Monitoring: Relationships with Self-Reports and Behavior Ratings" (paper presented at the Annual Meeting of the American Educational Research Association, Montreal, Quebec, Canada, April 1999), 9.

27. Schraw, "Promoting General Metacognitive Awareness," 4.

28. Ibid.

29. John Dewey, *How We Think: A Restatement of the Relation of Reflective Thinking to the Educative Process* (New York: D. C. Heath and Company, 1933), 78.

30. Pogonowski, "Metacognition: Musical Thinking," 11–12.

31. Dawson and Guare, *Smart but Scattered*, 275; Graham Foster, Evelyn Sawicki, Hyacinth Schaeffer, and Victor Zelinski, *I Think, Therefore I Learn!* (Markham, Ontario, Canada: Pembroke Publishers, 2002), 11; Gregory Schraw, "Promoting General Metacognitive Awareness," *Instructional Science* 26, no. 1–2 (1998): 118–21.

32. Dawson and Guare, *Smart but Scattered*, 232.

33. E. D. Hirsch Jr., *The Schools We Need and Why We Don't Have Them* (New York: Doubleday, 1996), 136–37.

34. Ibid., 139–42.

## 2

# METACOGNITION FOR MUSIC LEARNING

**M**usic education shares many elements in common with education in academic disciplines such as language, math, and science. Music educators know, however, that music teaching and learning are unique processes that cannot mimic other academic disciplines too closely without losing some of the core elements that make music teaching and learning most valid and meaningful. Music learning involves acquisition of knowledge and skill in cognitive, psychomotor, and affective domains of learning.

- *The cognitive domain.* Music learners must acquire content knowledge, deep understanding, and the ability to carry out analysis and synthesis in relation to their musical activities. These components of the music-learning process exist in the cognitive-learning domain. Knowledge, understanding, analysis, and synthesis are not enough, however, for music learners to develop the ability to perform music.
- *The psychomotor domain.* Music performance requires skills that are built in the psychomotor-learning domain. Depending on the performing medium, every music learner must acquire a myriad of motor skills along a continuum of increasingly complex and refined

abilities, all focused toward an end product of playing or singing excellently. Musical knowledge, skill, and ability would be pointless, however, without acquisition of deep understanding in the affective-learning domain.

- *The affective domain.* Because music is an art, many of the reasons for learning music lie within the affective domain of spirit, emotion, and desire to communicate with an audience. Music learning in the affective domain includes knowledge of appropriate performance practice, as well as understanding of musical expression and ability to shape sound in performance for artistically meaningful communication.

Let us consider an example of music learning in all three domains. Students in a high school band must have content knowledge related to techniques for playing their various instruments, including fingerings, breath control, and embouchure. Additionally, they must have content knowledge about reading music notation, such as pitch and rhythm reading, along with knowledge of key and meter signatures and marks of articulation and expression. While learning content knowledge, the band students are operating in the cognitive domain of learning. Psychomotor skills, related to playing their instruments, allow students to demonstrate their content knowledge in real music making. Hours of practice are spent on learning in the psychomotor domain as band members build performance skills for playing their instruments. But for many students it is the learning in the affective domain that cements their commitment to membership in the school band. The students'

---

**Tips for Teachers**

On the day after a concert performance, involve students in a discussion of the learning processes that led up to the event. Ask them to identify new knowledge and skills gained through preparation for performance and to describe their own growth as musicians. Ask students to share their perspectives on the value of working toward concert-performance goals. Find out what students are thinking about their practice and performance experiences.

**Photo 2.1.   High School Band, French Horns**

affective understanding of the spirit and emotion of the music, as well as a feeling of camaraderie with their peers and pride in their band, all culminate in meaningful communication with their audience through performance.

In this chapter, we will explore research on metacognition applied specifically to music learning and find that all three domains will be represented. Further, we will imagine some typical scenarios in which students apply metacognitive skills for music learning in the cognitive, psychomotor, and affective domains.

## OVERVIEW OF RESEARCH ON METACOGNITION IN MUSIC EDUCATION

Because most of the research on metacognition has been conducted in academic subject areas, music educators might feel that they must translate conclusions from academic disciplines into meaningful conclusions for teaching and learning the art of music. The problem with translating research findings from other disciplines into the context of music teaching and learning is that academic disciplines lack the complexity of interaction among cognitive knowledge, psychomotor skill, and expression of emotion that is crucial to music making. Thankfully, some music education researchers have addressed the topic of metacognition as a phenomenon specifically situated in music-learning contexts. The following overview provides a chronological sampling of some of the research on metacognition in music education, as presented in writings from the past three decades. Additionally, summaries of many more music education research studies are offered in subsequent chapters of this book.

### 1989—MENC Published *Dimensions of Musical Thinking*, in Which Metacognition was Recognized as One of the Dimensions of Musical Thinking.

Lenore Pogonowski contributed the chapter on metacognition, stating that learners might benefit from using metacognitive skills while performing, creating, and listening to music. She asserted that music learners can use metacognition to control their own learning processes, thereby achieving greater success than if they simply go about their music activities in a less aware, rote manner.[1]

## 1995—College Students in Musicianship Classes Benefitted from Using the Metacognitive Skills of Self-Awareness and Self-Reflection.

In an empirical study of university music students, Marilyn Egan investigated the effects of metacognition on student achievement in musicianship classes. Learners received instruction in how to apply metacognitive skills for maximizing their learning. Specifically, they learned to monitor and regulate their own learning processes by recognizing their perceptual learning-style preferences. Egan instructed participants to think about their own thinking and to understand if they were visual, aural, or kinesthetic learners. Then, using the metacognitive skills of self-monitoring and self-questioning, learners adapted their learning-style preferences to the learning tasks in musicianship classes. They were encouraged to plan their own learning and to develop personal learning strategies.[2] Egan provided questions as prompts for students' self-reflections regarding their learning tasks in musicianship classes. Participants in the study made significant gains in musicianship skills, leading Egan to conclude that metacognition had a positive effect on acquisition of knowledge and skill in musicianship classes.

## 1997—In an Empirical Study, Elementary School Music Students Used the Metacognitive Skill of Self-Assessment as a Tool for Developing Vocal Pitch-Matching Ability.

Sandra Mathias found that self-assessment led to significant gains in vocal-pitch accuracy among children who were initially inaccurate singers. Through playing matching games and then having children assess their own pitch-matching accuracy, Mathias found that 42 percent of first graders self-assessed accurately and that 63 percent of third through fifth graders self-assessed accurately. She concluded that the metacognitive skill of self-assessment had a positive effect on acquisition of vocal pitch–matching ability among elementary school children.[3]

## 1997—Metacognition, as a Self-Regulatory Skill, Was Encouraged Among At-Risk Male Students in a Choral-Music Program.

In a study designed to explore ways to help at-risk adolescent males develop increased self-efficacy, Darolyne Nelson encouraged participants to use metacognition in choral-music classes. Learners made gains in vocal-performance self-efficacy. Choral directors who implemented the study used metacognitive activities among students as a strategy to teach and reinforce higher-order thinking skills. They found that using higher-order thinking skills contributed to self-regulation, mental-preparation, and verbal-expression skills among their choral singers. Directors promoted metacognition through questioning techniques. They required learners to respond to questions such as "How do you know that?" and then to describe a personal plan of action for solving musical problems or correcting mistakes. According to Nelson, "questioning strategies consistently provided the learners with active engagement of cognitive skills. The boys were challenged not to simply sing but to think before and while they were singing . . . metacognition was often included in the [teaching] strategies."[4] Nelson concluded that metacognition had a positive effect on development of self-efficacy among at-risk teenage boys in the choral-music program.

## 2001—In an Investigative Study, Susan Hallam Compared the Habits of Novice and Expert Musicians and Found that Professional Musicians Routinely Used Metacognition to a Greater Degree than Their Novice Counterparts.

Musicians must use metacognitive skills for a variety of music-learning tasks. This is true of expert musicians as well as students. In fact, Hallam found that a defining characteristic of expert musicians, as compared to novices, was the degree to which they used metacognition in their approaches to practicing and performing. Hallam stated the following:

> A musician requires considerable metacognitive skills in order to be able to recognize the nature and requirements of a particular task; to identify particular difficulties; to have knowledge of a range of strategies for dealing with these problems; to know which strategy is appropriate for

tackling each task; to monitor progress towards the goal and, if progress is unsatisfactory, acknowledge this and draw on alternative strategies; [and] to evaluate learning outcomes in performance contexts and take action as necessary to improve performance in the future.[5]

Further, Hallam concluded that well-developed metacognitive skills allowed professional musicians to "learn to learn." Specifically, the professionals used metacognition to (1) identify personal strengths and weaknesses, (2) assess the difficulty of music to be learned, and (3) devise and apply strategies for optimal performance.[6]

## 2002—MENC Published *Dimensions of Musical Learning and Teaching: A Different Kind of Classroom*, a Follow-Up to the 1989 Book. Once Again, Metacognition was Cited as an Essential Type of Thinking for Music Learning.

Editor Eunice Boardman asserted that metacognition plays a "crucial role" in music learning. She advised music educators to regularly share information about thinking processes with their students. According to Boardman, students may use critical thinking, creative thinking, decision making, and problem solving in pursuit of music-learning goals. Metacognitive processes will emerge in music learners to the extent to which teachers make them aware of available types of thinking for music learning.[7]

## 2002—Metacognition was Promoted as a Beneficial Type of Thinking for Students in a High School Band Class.

In performance ensembles, such as choirs and bands, it is most often the case that directors maintain control of all aspects of rehearsals and performances at all times. There is good reason for this approach, as directors must ensure that performance quality is of the highest standard for their ensembles. Richard Kennell, however, suggested that high school band directors can promote metacognition among their players by sharing with them some of the directorial-control processes that are crucial to the success of the ensemble.

Directors can provide opportunities for band students to share in strategy planning and problem solving related to musical tasks and challenges. Thus, players can glimpse the planning processes of their directors. Additionally, they can begin to solve musical problems for themselves when the director challenges them to do so.[8] Kennell proposed that developing metacognition among band members might have a positive effect on the music-making ability of the ensemble.

## 2002—Researchers Warned Against Too Much Emphasis on Metacognition Among Music Students with Special Needs.

Welsbacher and Bernstorf encouraged music teachers of students with disabilities or cultural disadvantages to provide opportunities for their students to develop metacognition, but they warned that metacognitive awareness and self-monitoring might be out of reach for this population of students. Although the researchers acknowledged the importance and usefulness of metacognition, they suggested that students with special needs might be incapable of this type of thinking. Further, the researchers suggested that emphasis on metacognition might overload the cognitive-processing abilities of students with particular special needs.[9]

## 2006—Lisk Proposed Metacognition as a Central Aspect of His New Approach to Instrumental Ensemble–Rehearsal Procedures.

In his book *The Creative Director: Conductor, Teacher, Leader*, Edward Lisk espoused his A.R.T. system (alternative rehearsal techniques). Lisk stated that: "*A.R.T. is a new dimension in teaching, thinking, practicing, and playing an instrument.* It is a departure from traditional instrumental techniques—a new paradigm for musical learning that recognizes the importance of metacognition."[10] Lisk encouraged directors to teach their instrumentalists how to use metacognition in rehearsals. He explained that "by actively engaging their musical minds, we develop their performance skills and teach them to make intelligent musical decisions through which they will more fully experience the entire world of musical masterworks."[11]

## 2006—Metacognitive Skills Were Promoted as Part of a Constructivist Approach to Teaching Music.

Focusing on the relationship between constructivist learning theories and music teaching and learning, Sheila Scott proposed that metacognition is an integral part of a constructivist view of music education. Scott observed that metacognition plays an essential part in students' ability to construct knowledge and meaning from musical experiences.[12] As music learners use metacognitive skills to construct musical understanding, they engage in reflective thinking and work toward solving their own musical problems. For this reason, Scott asserted that metacognitive skills and the child-centered activities of a constructivist music classroom go hand in hand.[13]

## 2007—Metacognition Emerged as an Important Factor when Hanna Examined the Revised Bloom's Taxonomy and Proposed Its Implications for Music Education.

Since the 1950s, educators in music and other academic areas have used Bloom's taxonomy of educational objectives to plan curricula, deliver instruction, and assess learning. In 2001, a revised version of Bloom's taxonomy was published. Most notably, the revised taxonomy features metacognition as one of four major *types of knowledge*. Applying the revised taxonomy to music education, Hanna affirmed the benefits of metacognition to music learners:

> In music learning, a key aspect of metacognition is strategic knowledge, which is vital to musical refinement. The ability to skillfully interpret music demands a high degree of self-knowledge. For example, many strategies that are formed during the development of musicianship are idiosyncratic and private; only the individual musician is privy to which strategies work for him or her. . . . Developing metacognition can help music learners to become more objective about their overall musicianship. If learners lack metacognition—that is, if learners are not able "to think about musical thinking"—their musicianship will plateau and fail to progress.[14]

## 2010—In an Investigative Study, Metacognition Emerged as a Beneficial Type of Thinking for Students in One-To-One Violin Lessons.

Graham McPhail conducted a study in which he promoted meta-cognition among students in one-to-one violin lessons. McPhail found that music teaching and learning were enriched when he consciously employed teaching strategies that helped students to develop meta-cognition. Specifically, McPhail required his violin students to monitor their own learning processes, recognize errors, identify problems, and create their own strategies to overcome difficulties. Teaching strategies included having students engage in self-reflection, self-evaluation, and awareness of personal strengths and weaknesses. As a result, the violin students became more self-regulated in their approach to learning and playing music. McPhail concluded that the use of metacognitive skills related to violin playing had a positive effect on students' progress in one-to-one lessons.[15]

## 2010—Scott Emphasized Metacognitive Activities as Part of a "Minds-On" Approach to Music Teaching.

Describing a "minds-on" approach to learning in the general-music classroom, Sheila Scott advised teachers that music learners should engage in several activities requiring metacognition: (1) self-reflection through journal writing, (2) self-assessment, (3) self-strategizing for learning, and (4) interaction with learning partners.

Without specifically using the term *metacognition*, Scott detailed a number of metacognitive teaching and learning strategies for the music classroom. She defined *minds-on learning* in this way: "Students actively construct musical knowledge for themselves by thinking about what they are currently doing in relation to what they already know."[16] This requires that students are self-aware and that they reflect on previous learning, and it precludes at least a modicum of self-assessment on the part of students. Self-awareness, reflection, and self-assessment are components of metacognition.

By contrast, Scott stated that *minds-off learning* occurs when "students complete tasks without thinking about what they are doing; they passively accept information provided by others."[17] Music educators might observe this type of minds-off learning among some of their students and endeavor to use teaching strategies that produce a learning environment where richer and deeper learning takes place.

## MANIFESTATIONS OF METACOGNITION IN MUSIC LEARNING

Because it is a thinking skill, metacognition is naturally a rather covert activity. In any music class, various students will use metacognition to greater or lesser degrees. On the surface, at any given moment, it might not be apparent that some students are using metacognition while others are not. It is noted, however, that with regard to self-awareness and self-regulatory behavior, students who use metacognition in their music learning are likely to progress more successfully than those who engage in music activities by rote, with little or no deep understanding of themselves as musicians. Metacognitive music learners develop self-awareness and begin to acknowledge their ability to construct musical meaning for themselves rather than always looking to a teacher or textbook for step-by-step directions.[18]

### Four Levels of Metacognition

It is likely that anyone reading this book uses metacognition at various times to accomplish learning goals. To be aware of one's thought processes and exert control over those processes in pursuit of learning is to use metacognition. It is likely, too, that readers sometimes engage in self-reflection and self-evaluation regarding the products of their efforts to learn new information, to solve problems, or to acquire and refine desired skills. Readers who are teachers might be reminded of students who appear to use metacognition on a regular basis to achieve learning goals and other students who appear to engage in metacognition to a lesser degree. Swartz and Perkins delineated four levels of metacognition, as follows:

1. *Tacit use.* The individual does a kind of thinking—say, decision making—without thinking about it.

2. *Aware use.* The individual does that kind of thinking conscious *that* and *when* he is doing so.
3. *Strategic use.* The individual organizes his or her thinking by way of particular conscious strategies that enhance its efficacy.
4. *Reflective use.* The individual reflects on his or her thinking before and after—or even in the middle of—the process, pondering how to proceed and how to improve.[19]

It is the premise of this book that many music educators will want to raise the levels of metacognition among their students from tacit use to aware, strategic, and reflective use.

## Metacognition and the National Standards for Music Education

The National Association for Music Education has developed the following national standards for music education[20]:

1. Singing, alone and with others, a varied repertoire of music
2. Performing on instruments, alone and with others, a varied repertoire of music

**Photo 2.2.   High School–Choir Rehearsal**

3. Improvising melodies, variations, and accompaniments
4. Composing and arranging music within specified guidelines
5. Reading and notating music
6. Listening to, analyzing, and describing music
7. Evaluating music and music performances
8. Understanding relationships between music, the other arts, and disciplines outside the arts
9. Understanding music in relation to history and culture

Music teachers can encourage students to use metacognitive skills as they pursue achievement of objectives related to all nine standards. While planning and delivering instruction, teachers can incorporate instructional strategies that promote metacognition in standards-based music curricula. Throughout this book, we will explore some of those instructional strategies along with the research that provides a foundation for understanding this type of instructional approach.

## SCENARIOS: METACOGNITION IN MUSIC TEACHING AND LEARNING

Some questions come to mind regarding metacognition among students in music classes. What does it look like? In what ways do music learners use metacognition? What are the overt actions of music learners when they are using metacognition? It may be helpful for music educators to consider the following scenarios in which music learners engage in metacognition.

---

**Tips for Teachers**

Resist the temptation to always "fix" mistakes for students. Instead, ask students to identify a mistake. Then, ask them to suggest strategies for correcting the mistake. Give students a chance to work through the problem for themselves. Then, if necessary, proceed to help students fix the mistake. The process appears to be time consuming, but it is important to provide opportunities for students to solve problems independently.

## Metacognition in Independent Practice

Metacognition is manifested in personal goal setting, situated in either long-term or short-term contexts. For example, let us imagine a piano student who sits down to begin a one-hour practice session. He mentally scans his goals for the week. Currently, he is working on three pieces of repertoire, and his teacher has assigned several scales, cadences, and arpeggios. Assessing his current strengths and weaknesses related to technique and repertoire, the student thinks of specific places in his music that need attention. Knowing that he has only an hour to devote to piano practice at this time, he decides that he will spend ten minutes on fingering, technique, and speed for one of his four-octave scales, working in both parallel and contrary motion. Then, he will turn his attention to the *B* section of a piece where he needs to count out some tricky rhythms, followed by some slow practice to solidify a technically difficult arpeggio section in another piece. Having made these decisions, the student begins practicing, knowing that he will be able to accomplish his goals within the allotted hour of practice time.

Along with goal setting, the piano student exhibits metacognition through self-awareness. He is aware of the amount of work he needs to do to accomplish his goals. Additionally, the piano student displays the ability to assess his own strengths and weaknesses regarding his current technique and repertoire. Armed with self-assessment, the student is able to focus on passages of music where he needs the most practice and not waste his time playing through passages that do not need his attention at this time. Awareness of time limitations in planning the one-hour practice session is further evidence of metacognition in that the metacognitive learner typically assesses available time and resources for accomplishing learning goals.

## Metacognition in a Choral-Music Rehearsal

Metacognition is manifested in devising and applying strategies for learning. When learners devise their own strategies for solving problems, they become less dependent on their teachers.

Let us imagine that an alto in a high school madrigal group realizes that she has trouble finding her pitch at a particular entrance in an a cappella piece. Frequently, in rehearsals, she misses her pitch at that entrance and becomes disoriented. She then notices that the basses sing her pitch in a lower octave just two beats before her entrance. Thereafter, just before her entrance she consciously tells herself to listen for the basses' note. Her strategy pays off, and she is able to accurately sing her pitch at the alto entrance. In subsequent rehearsals and performances, as long as she applies her strategy, the singer never again has a pitch problem at that point in the music.

In addition to devising and applying an appropriate strategy to solve a problem, this student exhibits the metacognitive skill of self-assessment. In order to know that she has a problem and needs to apply a strategy to solve it, the learner must first use self-assessment to be aware of her weakness in finding the correct pitch.

## Metacognition in a Music-Theory Class

Metacognition is manifested in awareness of personal strengths and weaknesses, related to music-learning tasks. Imagine a student in a beginning music theory class who is being introduced to ear training. She finds that her aural analysis of triads is very good. She is almost always accurate in identifying major, minor, diminished, and augmented triads via aural perception. She realizes, however, that she is much less accurate when trying to identify intervals. Acknowledging that aural interval identification is a weakness, she determines to spend more time and practice on developing this skill.

The student's self-awareness of strengths and weaknesses in aural skills is most likely based on feedback from her teacher as well as her own self-assessment. Because of self-awareness, she then determines to actively take steps to solve the problem of her weakness in aural interval identification.

## Metacognition in the Band

Metacognition is manifested in self-reflection. Consider an example of members of a middle school band engaging in self-reflection. First, they spend months learning and polishing repertoire for performance in an adjudicated festival. Following the important performance event, their director assigns a journal-writing project in which students are asked to write responses to several questions posed by the director:

1. In what ways are you a better musician because of practicing, rehearsing, and performing for the festival?
2. Describe your personal strengths and weaknesses in performing for the festival.
3. Describe the strengths and weaknesses of the whole band in performing for the festival.
4. In what ways did your experiences of practicing, rehearsing, and performing for the festival add to your feelings of pride in our band?

As students work on the journal-writing assignment, they remember their efforts and preparations over the past several months as well as the excitement of the final performance. The reflection project allows them to assign meaning to their experiences. By creating the journaling project, the band director implies that students are responsible for constructing their own growing musicianship and placing their own values on band membership and activities.

After the journal entries have been submitted, the band director reads the student reflections, writes brief messages in the margins, and returns journals to the band members. This small gesture of recognition and communication from director to students is a valuable tool for developing positive rapport and morale in the performing ensemble.

The band director accomplishes several goals through this assignment. He or she provides writing prompts that require his students to (1) increase awareness of themselves as musicians, (2) assess their personal strengths and weaknesses as well as those of the ensemble, and (3) reflect on matters in the affective domain, including feelings of pride in their accomplishments. Due to variety in the writing prompts provided by their director, students are able to exercise metacognitive skills, including self-awareness and self-assessment. Additionally, it is likely that students' good feelings about belonging to the band are reinforced when their director responds by writing messages in the margins of their journals.

## SUGGESTIONS FOR MUSIC TEACHERS

Based on evidence from music education research, subsequent chapters in this book will present ideas for music educators to incorporate into their teaching some instructional strategies for promoting metacognition among their students. An attempt is made to include information that will be useful for music teachers on a variety of grade levels and in a variety of types of music instruction. The intention is to inspire creative music educators to create their own innovative teaching strategies that expand on what is offered here.

## NOTES

1. Lenore Pogonowski, "Metacognition: A Dimension of Musical Thinking," in *Dimensions of Musical Thinking*, edited by Eunice Boardman (Reston, Va.: MENC, 1989), 11.

2. Marilyn M. Egan, "Effects of Metacognition on Music Achievement of University Students" (Ph.D. diss., Kent State University, ProQuest, UMI Dissertations Publishing, 1995, 9536648), 4.

3. Sandra L. Mathias, "A Teaching Technique to Aid the Development of Vocal Accuracy in Elementary School Students" (Ph.D. diss., Ohio State University, UMI Dissertations Publishing, 1997, 9735675), 65.

4. Darolyne L. Nelson, "High-Risk Adolescent Males, Self-Efficacy, and Choral Performance: An Investigation of Affective Intervention" (DMA diss., Arizona State University, ProQuest, UMI Dissertations Publishing, 1997, 9725321), 425.

5. Susan Hallam, "The Development of Metacognition in Musicians: Implications for Education," *British Journal of Music Education* 4, no. 1 (2001): 28.

6. Ibid., 37.

7. Eunice Boardman, "The Relationship of Musical Thinking and Learning to Classroom Instruction," in *Dimensions of Musical Learning and Teaching: A Different Kind of Classroom*, edited by Eunice Boardman (Reston, Va.: MENC, 2002), 18.

8. Richard Kennell, "Musical Thinking in the Instrumental Rehearsal," in *Dimensions of Musical Thinking*, edited by Eunice Boardman (Reston, Va.: MENC, 2002), 189–91.

9. Betty T. Welsbacher and Elaine D. Bernstorf, "Musical Thinking among Diverse Students," in *Dimensions of Musical Learning and Teaching: A Different Kind of Classroom*, edited by Eunice Boardman (Reston, Va.: MENC, 2002), 158.

10. Edward Lisk, *The Creative Director: Conductor, Teacher, Leader* (Galesville, Md.: Meredith Music Publications, 2006), 306 (Kindle book).

11. Ibid., 313–14.

12. Sheila Scott, "A Constructivist View of Music Education: Perspectives for Deep Learning," *General Music Today* 19, no. 2 (2006): 17.

13. Ibid., 19.

14. Wendell Hanna, "The New Bloom's Taxonomy: Implications for Music Education," *Arts Education Policy Review* 108, no. 4 (2007): 14.

15. Graham J. McPhail, "Crossing Boundaries: Sharing Concepts of Music Teaching from Classroom to Studio," *Music Education Research* 12, no. 1 (2010): 33–45.

16. Sheila Scott, "A Minds-On Approach to Active Learning in General Music," *General Music Today* 24, no. 1 (2010): 24.

17. Ibid.

18. Pogonowski, "Metacognition," 9.

19. Robert J. Swartz and D. N. Perkins, *Teaching Thinking: Issues and Approaches* (Pacific Grove, Calif.: Midwest Publications, 1990), 52.

20. National Association for Music Education, "National Standards for Music Education," http://musiced.nafme.org/resources/national-standards-for-music-education/ (accessed August 4, 2013).

# 3

# METACOGNITION AND SELF-REGULATION FOR MUSIC LEARNING

The success of music learners on all levels from beginner through professional is built on self-regulation. Metacognition is necessary for self-monitoring, leading to self-regulation, and this ability appears to develop commensurately with expertise. Being self-aware of strengths and weaknesses, recognizing problems, and knowing how to apply strategies to solve problems and correct errors are abilities that are noticeably greater among expert musicians than novices.[1] Of course, music educators generally spend their time and energy working with novice musicians rather than experts. Although they recognize that students are not experts, it is a goal of music educators to facilitate their students' progress along a continuum of achievement from the novice to the expert level.

Self-regulation involves control of self. Metacognition provides a basis for self-regulation in that it involves awareness of oneself as a learner. Using that awareness, metacognitive learners exert self-regulation to control their thought processes along with their learning activities.[2] According to Zimmerman, "self-regulation refers to self-generated thoughts, feelings, and actions that are planned and cyclically adapted to the attainment of personal goals."[3] Furthermore, self-regulation involves personal, behavioral, and environmental processes. Self-regulating learners observe their own learning processes, adjust their learning behaviors, and assess environmental conditions or outcomes.[4] In music, this translates to awareness of one's own musical thought processes, adjustment of one's own music-practice or -performance behaviors, and assessment of one's own music-performance outcomes.

The abilities to self-monitor and then to correct one's own errors are metacognitive skills that result in self-regulation.[5] Welsbacher and Bernstorf proposed that artists da Vinci and Matisse became "world-changers," in part because they possessed the metacognitive qualities of self-awareness and self-monitoring.[6] Music educators are probably not concerned with whether their students will become world-changers; however, they are most definitely concerned with student success in music learning. In the early years of metacognition research, Flavell stated his belief that metacognitive self-monitoring aids students in pursuit of learning: "I find it hard to believe that children who do more cognitive monitoring would not learn better both in and out of school than children who do less. I also think that increasing the quantity and quality of children's metacognitive knowledge and monitoring skills through systematic training may be feasible as well as desirable."[7]

Self-regulation involves metacognition, motivation, behavioral processes, and a sense of self-efficacy.[8] When music educators encourage their students to use metacognitive skills for self-regulation, they set the stage for lifelong learning by increasing student autonomy.[9] Thus learners begin to make progress when working independently and do not wait to be directed by their teachers regarding every little step in the learning process.

Self-regulation is inherent in higher-order thinking skills. Presseisen stated that "higher-order thinking means self-regulation of the thinking process. We do not recognize higher-order thinking in an individual when someone else 'calls the plays' at every step."[10] Self-regulated learners do not need to wait for their teachers to "call the plays" when they use metacognition to plan, monitor, and evaluate their own learning.

It may be argued that self-regulation is even more important in music learning than in other academic areas. Self-regulation is vital to success, as participation in music activities is frequently a voluntary choice on the part of the learner. Music classes, one-to-one lessons, and participation in performance ensembles are often elective courses or extracurricular activities, requiring students to take initiative and independent action in pursuit of musical goals.[11] Furthermore, self-regulated music practice away from the classroom is critical for development of basic musicianship among beginning and intermediate music students, such as those in middle and high school bands; and success in the initial, formative phases is crucial for retention of students in performing ensembles.[12] Consequently, self-regulation is not only important in initial phases of music participation but also crucial for retaining competent young musicians who continue to make progress toward musical excellence in performing ensembles.

## METACOGNITION FOR SELF-REGULATION

The concepts of metacognition and self-regulation are inextricably intertwined. Metacognition is a necessary component of self-regulation, and it is through metacognition that self-regulation becomes possible. At the same time, it can be said that self-regulation is a component of metacognition, particularly with regard to controlling thought processes.

### Metacognitive Knowledge: Declarative, Procedural, and Conditional

The ability to self-regulate in a learning situation is dependent on several factors, as follows:

- *Self-awareness.* Metacognitive learners are able to step back and look at themselves, considering what they are thinking and doing.
- *Metacognitive declarative knowledge.* Learners know about their own thought processes and are, therefore, aware of their strengths and weaknesses related to learning tasks. They are aware of what they know from previous experience and what they do not know but need to know. This basic knowledge about themselves as learners provides a foundation from which metacognitive learners can effectively work on learning tasks.
- *Metacognitive procedural knowledge.* Because they are aware of their thinking processes, metacognitive learners understand what they will need to do in order to accomplish learning tasks. They

are able to devise and apply strategies that will help them achieve their learning goals.

- *Metacognitive conditional knowledge.* Metacognitive learners not only know some effective strategies for learning, but they also know when, why, and how to apply those strategies.[13]

Let us consider a scenario in which a learner applies metacognitive declarative, procedural, and conditional knowledge for music learning. A first grader in a general-music class becomes aware of how it sounds and how it feels when she claps patterns of eighth notes and quarter notes with her teacher. Through experience, she recognizes that she sometimes matches her teacher perfectly but, at other times, her clapping is not the same as her teacher's. She observes that eighth notes are connected by a beam while quarter notes are not. She remembers that the teacher taught her to say the word *apple* when reading and clapping a pair of eighth notes and to say the word *pear* when reading and clapping quarter notes. She applies this strategy, remembering which

**Photo 3.1. Kindergarten Xylophones**

notes should sound like *apple* and which notes should sound like *pear*. Because the learner understands when and why to apply the "apple/pear" strategy, she is accurate in reading and clapping rhythm patterns. Based on self-awareness and metacognitive declarative knowledge, the learner uses metacognitive procedural and conditional knowledge to achieve success in music class.

## Planning, Monitoring, and Evaluating

The metacognitive skills of planning, monitoring, and evaluating allow learners to put metacognitive knowledge into self-regulatory action.[14]

- *Planning.* The learner plans for learning by selecting and allocating resources, budgeting time, selecting learning strategies, being aware of personal strengths and weaknesses from previous learning experiences, and setting goals for new learning.
- *Monitoring.* The act of monitoring learning refers to ongoing self-awareness and self-assessment throughout a learning task, including repetition, correction, revision, or redirection when needed and revision of goals when needed.
- *Evaluating.* Finally, the learner engages in self-evaluation by assessing outcomes at the end of a learning task. Self-evaluation allows the learner to prepare for the next round of learning in which the learner will need to start with an awareness of personal strengths and weaknesses, based on self-evaluation.

McPherson and Zimmerman identified three phases of the "self-regulated learning cycle" giving the names (1) forethought, (2) performance and volition control, and (3) self-reflection to the phases that are labeled by other researchers as planning, monitoring, and evaluating.[15] In the forethought phase, the learner engages in task analysis, setting goals, and planning strategies. In the performance and volition-control phase, the learner engages in metacognitive monitoring and application of strategies for solving problems, as well as detecting and correcting errors. In the self-reflection phase, the learner engages in self-evaluation. This sets in motion the self-regulatory cycle for the next learning task.

Imagine the following scenario in which a collegiate voice student applies self-regulatory metacognitive skills. In the planning (forethought) phase, the voice student selects a Schubert lied to prepare for an upcoming recital. She uses metacognition as she is aware of her own ability level, her strengths and weaknesses, and her goals. The student peruses the score and listens to a recording to determine if the piece will be in her vocal range and within her technical capabilities. She also considers whether she has sufficient time to prepare the piece to performance-readiness by the date of the recital. During the monitoring phase (also called the performance and volition-control phase), the student completes numerous practice sessions. During each session, she uses metacognitive skills to (1) set goals, (2) detect and correct errors, (3) apply effective strategies for technical and artistic aspects of performing the piece, and (4) evaluate her progress as she refines her skill. Finally, the day of the recital arrives, and the student is ready to perform the Schubert lied. Following her performance, she enters the self-evaluation (self-reflection) phase. Based on personal feedback and on feedback from audience members and her voice professor, the student makes a self-evaluation of her performance. This self-evaluation, in turn, provides metacognitive declarative knowledge that will aid the student in the planning (forethought) phase for the next piece in her repertoire. In this scenario, the three phases—(1) planning (forethought), (2) monitoring (performance and volition control), (3) and self-evaluation (self-reflection)—can be observed on a large scale throughout the project. The three phases can also be observed on a small scale within each practice session, leading up to the recital performance. The application of metacognitive skills for self-regulation is apparent throughout the planning, monitoring, and evaluation phases of the voice student's project.

---

### Tips for Teachers

When introducing a new skill or a new piece of music, ask students to tell you the procedures that they will use to accomplish the new learning. Find out their thoughts, and then fill in suggestions where needed. Emphasize the sequential, step-by-step nature of practicing new musical skills or repertoire. Encourage students to monitor their own progress as they work through the new learning.

# OVERVIEW OF RESEARCH ON SELF-REGULATION IN MUSIC LEARNING

Much of the research on self-regulation in music learning has been conducted in the area of independent music practice, such as when learners practice playing their instruments at home, away from their teachers. This topic will be explored further in chapter 7, Metacognition for Independent Music-Practice Sessions. A brief, chronological overview of some of the research on self-regulation in music learning is provided here.

## 1989—In a Case Study, a Piano Student Optimized Practice Time by Applying Metacognitive Skills.

Kacper Miklaszewski studied the practice habits and behaviors of a gifted young piano student who subsequently became a concert pianist. At the time of the study, while still a student, the pianist exhibited a high degree of systematic strategy use during practice. Strategies included breaking the music down into short fragments, alternating fast and slow practice of sections of music, splicing together longer sections after intense practice of short fragments, and writing in the score. The pianist was able to administer effective strategies because he maintained self-awareness, monitored his practice, and engaged in ongoing self-evaluation. Thus, his successful self-regulation was based on application of metacognitive skills.[16]

## 1997—In Another Case Study, Metacognitive Skills Emerged as Crucial Factors in the Self-Regulated Practice Habits of an Organ Student.

Siw Nielsen studied the practice habits of a twenty-one-year-old organ student preparing a piece for performance. He recorded the student's practice sessions and verbal reports and comments made during those sessions. According to Nielsen, "*self-regulation* refers to learners being active participants in their own learning process. . . . Learners' use of learning strategies involves making choices between different strategies depending on the task, characteristics of the individual, and dimensions in the learning situation."[17]

Nielsen found that much of the organ student's success depended on applying metacognitive skills as follows: (1) the student recognized technical problems when they occurred, (2) the student self-evaluated throughout his practice sessions, and (3) when a problem occurred, the student applied a strategy to correct the problem. The organ student applied conditional, metacognitive knowledge by deciding when, where, and how to apply strategies.[18] Most of the strategies involved isolation and repetition of technically difficult passages in the music. Thus, the organ student made productive use of metacognitive procedural and conditional knowledge during practice sessions.

Nielsen viewed the type of learning that takes place during individual practice sessions as strategic processing applied to problem solving, necessary for making progress. The organ student's self-evaluations relied partly on criteria that he had defined in accordance with his anticipated final performance (the outcome) and also on criteria based on attainable levels of performance in progressive phases of practice. Therefore, the student's interpretation of weak spots also appeared to involve his available metacognitive knowledge.[19] Because the student was self-aware regarding personal strengths and weaknesses as measured against the anticipated final performance outcome, he was able to apply problem-solving strategies in practice sessions to reach his final performance goal.

## 1997—In an Empirical Study, Students with Abilities to Monitor and Control their Music Practice Demonstrated Higher Achievement than Those with Lesser Metacognitive Abilities.

The ability to devise and apply strategies for learning is a metacognitive skill. Gary McPherson studied music learners' use of three musical behaviors that may be employed during independent practice: (1) playing by ear, (2) playing from memory, and (3) improvising. These three skills provided a "range of activities"[20] for music students to use while practicing. When students were tested on their ability to engage in the three musical behaviors, McPherson found that those students who displayed metacognitive ability also received the highest scores on the tests. By contrast, the weakest students did not have the ability to monitor and control their practicing and were therefore unable to overcome encountered problems. Hence, the students who received lower scores on music-performance tests were those who displayed less ability to apply metacognitive skills for self-regulation during practice.[21]

## 2001—In a Longitudinal Study, Researchers Found that Beginning Band Students Were Hampered in Self-Regulatory Skills by the Physical Challenges of Handling their Instruments; However, Those Who Did Employ Metacognitive Self-Regulation Demonstrated Higher-Achieving Progress.

McPherson and Renwick studied individual music practice over a three-year period among a group of children who were beginning instrumental music students. The research method focused on *how* the children practiced with regard to applied practice strategies. The researchers identified and studied six "dimensions" of self-regulatory behavior relative to musical practice as follows:

1. *Motive.* Feeling free to and capable of deciding whether to practice.
2. *Method.* Planning and applying suitable strategies when practicing.
3. *Time.* Consistency of practice and time management.
4. *Performance outcomes.* Monitoring, evaluating, and controlling performance.
5. *Physical environment.* Structuring the practice environment (e.g., away from distractions).
6. *Social factors.* Actively seeking information that might assist (e.g., from another family member, teacher, practice diary, or method book).[22]

McPherson and Renwick found that, while these six self-regulatory processes typically comprise distinguishing characteristics of expert practice, they were also seen in practice behaviors of young, beginning band students. The researchers observed self-regulatory behaviors to greater and lesser degrees among subjects, with patterns emerging in various learners. Those who employed self-regulation in individual practice were able to make higher-achieving progress in music.

Some beginning students in McPherson and Renwick's study found it difficult to monitor their own playing because they faced psychomotor challenges of handling and coordinating the playing of their instruments. Those children who did monitor their own playing were able to detect errors. When they corrected errors rather than ignoring them, their rate of achievement was higher than that of their peers. These results implied that self-monitoring followed by planning and implementing strategies for self-correction were critical metacognitive skills for music learning among participants in the study.[23]

### 2001—In a Case Study, Organ Students Exhibited the Metacognitive Skills of Planning, Self-Monitoring, and Self-Assessment During Practice Sessions.

Siw Nielsen studied practice behaviors of two advanced organ students and observed self-regulatory practice behaviors occurring in three phases: (1) forethought (planning before or early on during practice), (2) performance control (self-monitoring during practice), and (3) self-reflection (self-assessment after practicing, which in turn informed the organists for the planning stages of subsequent practice sessions).[24] According to Nielsen, students demonstrated self-regulation in learning by doing the following: (1) setting specific goals, (2) engaging in strategic planning, and (3) using self-instruction, self-control, self-monitoring, and self-judgment.

### 2006—Strategy Use, Based on Self-Awareness and Self-Assessment, Emerged as an Effective Practice Tool for College Brass Players.

We have established that strategizing is an important metacognitive skill. When learners become aware of problems or challenges in self-regulated-learning tasks, they must develop strategies to deal with the problems. Or learners may apply strategies that have been suggested by their teachers. In an investigative study, Peter Miksza observed and recorded practice behaviors among forty college brass players and measured their practice effectiveness. Players who were less impulsive attained greater proficiency through more effective practice because they more frequently applied strategies to resolve difficulties while practicing.[25] Miksza concluded that "brass players should approach their practicing more strategically in order to be more effective."[26]

## 2008—Participants In an Exploratory Study Demonstrated the Effectiveness of Self-Monitoring and Self-Evaluation in Music Practice.

In a study of practice habits of a group of college music majors, Byo and Cassidy found that metacognitive, self-regulatory skills aided students in structuring effective individual practice sessions. For maximum effectiveness, learners needed to be self-aware regarding personal skill levels as compared with the difficulty of music to be practiced.

Additionally, Byo and Cassidy found that successful learners devised and applied effective practice strategies while monitoring their own concentration levels. The researchers found that "self-regulation . . . is characterized by a cyclic process of self-monitoring, self-evaluating, and adaptive behavior in the learner's ongoing pursuit of a goal. Metacognition and self-regulation acknowledge the conditional, not fixed, nature of practice and are evident in the practice of advanced and novice performers."[27]

## 2008—In an Exploratory Study, Middle School Students Demonstrated Metacognitive Skills for Instrumental Music Practice.

It is known that expert musicians engage in (1) planning, (2) identifying problems, (3) devising and applying strategies to correct problems, and (4) self-evaluation during practice sessions. Amanda Leon-Guerrero studied the practice habits of middle school band students and identified their self-regulatory behaviors as occurring in three categories, similar to behaviors of expert musicians: (1) problem recognition, (2) strategy selection, and (3) evaluation of performance.[28]

According to Leon-Guerrero, "practice is a fundamental expectation of every music lesson, whether it is as an individual or in a group. Similar to studying; it is the musicians' way of self-learning outside of the classroom or rehearsal."[29] Leon-Guerrero concluded that promoting self-regulation in independent music practice might be a way for teachers to improve music learning among their students.

## 2012—A Test to Measure the Dimensions of Self-Regulation Among Music Students was Introduced.

In 2011, McPherson and Zimmerman reasserted the six dimensions of self-regulation[30] (as introduced by McPherson and Renwick in 2001).

These are motive, method, time, performance outcomes, physical environment, and social factors. In 2012, Mikszo published "preliminary evidence of predictive validity"[31] of a test to measure these specific dimensions: motive/self-efficacy, method and behavior, time management, and social influences as related to music learners' self-regulated practice. According to Mikszo, the measure may prove to be useful to music educators and researchers who want to determine the degree to which their students use self-regulation in independent music practice.

## 2012—Researchers Measured Three Dimensions of Self-Regulation Among Middle and Junior High School Band Students.

Mikszo, Prichard, and Sorbo measured methods, behaviors, and time use among intermediate instrumental students during independent practice. The researchers defined these dimensions. "The *method* dimension," they said, "refers to selection and application of both physical and mental learning strategies, whereas the *behavior* dimension essentially refers to individuals' abilities to self-evaluate and monitor their own learning. The *time-use* dimension refers to elements such as concentration and organization of time usage. . . . Taken together, the method, behavior, and time-use dimensions represent issues of resource management, metacognitive-strategy use, and adaptive-learning strategies in general."[32]

Results showed that participants tended to work almost exclusively on note accuracy and to play through long passages of music rather than breaking the music down into smaller fragments. Additionally, participants tended to engage in longer practice frames at the beginning of their practice sessions. Based on these results, the researchers asserted the importance of music teachers modeling productive practice habits for their students.[33]

## A DEVELOPMENTAL PERSPECTIVE ON METACOGNITION AND SELF-REGULATION

Music educators reading this chapter may be wondering about realistic expectations regarding age or grade levels of students who are able to self-regulate in music learning. Adolescent and adult learners do exhibit greater capacity for using metacognition and self-regulation than do children.[34] It is possible, however, to structure learning so that younger children may also begin to develop these skills.[35] "Inner language" is thought to be a prerequisite for metacognition, and it begins in most children around age five. The type of thinking that might be affirmatively labeled *metacognition* does not fully develop, however, until approximately age eleven. This is the age at which children are generally capable of formal thought.[36]

Metacognition, as a component of self-regulation, is exercised when learners are challenged to monitor their own learning and solve their own problems. Davidson and Scripp proposed that productive instructional environments are those that place children in situations where cognitive conflicts, or challenges, are presented. They found that "learning occurs with the development of problem-solving strategies required for resolving cognitive conflicts in the environment."[37] Therefore, to the extent that children are developmentally ready to apply strategies for working out challenges or difficulties in music making, they are ready to use metacognition for self-regulating their music learning.

## TEACHING SELF-REGULATION TO MUSIC LEARNERS

As stated previously, researchers studying self-regulation in music learning have focused primarily on independent practice. It is not enough for teachers to simply make assignments in repertoire and technique and then tell students to go home and practice. It is important for teachers to instruct students in *how* to practice. Beginners

---

**Tips for Teachers**

Before a student leaves a one-to-one music lesson, ask the student to explain at least one musical goal for the week and to describe the practice strategies that will be necessary to achieving that goal. When the student returns for the next lesson, introduce a discussion of whether the student was able to employ the anticipated strategies to accomplish the goal for the past week.

must be taught to break down their music into achievable fragments, such as repetitively practicing the first eight measures of a beginner étude before going on to the next eight measures. Even intermediate learners must be taught technical strategies, such as a pianist practicing running passages with staccato articulation when the final goal is legato clarity or a singer practicing melodic intervals of a song on the syllable *loo* before adding text.

Additionally, it is often advantageous for music learners to use self-regulatory skills while engaged in music classes with other learners, such as when students work independently in small groups, when singers or instrumentalists divide into sectional rehearsals, or when performers function together in an ensemble. Based on ideas presented in this chapter, the following list presents instructional strategies for teachers who want to help their music learners develop metacognitive, self-regulatory skills.

## Build Self-Regulation into Independent Group Work

In an elementary general-music class, students may work in small groups to compose simple melodies, create rhythm patterns on classroom instruments, construct soundscapes, complete notation-reading or -writing assignments, or accomplish any number of other creative music-learning activities. When placing students in small groups for projects, the music educator has a wonderful opportunity to encourage self-regulation. In addition to making an assignment, the teacher can map out a set of steps that allows students to self-regulate. For example, the teacher might instruct that Step 1 will consist of learners planning their own goals for the project, choosing and organizing materials, and taking note of the amount of time allotted for completion of the project. Step 2 will consist of learners devising and applying a strategy for completing the project, monitoring their own progress, evaluating whether the work comes close to the original goal, and keeping an eye on the time. Step 3 will consist of learners self-evaluating the success of their projects in finished form. In some situations, this final step will come after presentation of a performance for the class. Personal feedback and feedback from the teacher and classmates will inform learners regarding their relative success, but emphasis should be placed on self-evaluation. Through a process of giving clear instructions regarding step-by-step procedures and then monitoring the whole class, the music educator can help learners to develop metacognitive, self-regulatory habits.

## Build Self-Regulation into Independent Music Practice

Music teachers often require at-home practice, especially for instrumental music students. Frequently, students are required to turn in practice logs. Figure 3.1 shows a page from a practice log in which self-regulation is built into the assignment.

<table>
<tr><td colspan="2" align="center">Practice Log</td></tr>
<tr><td>Name _____</td><td>Date _____</td></tr>
<tr><td colspan="2">Assigned Scales: _____</td></tr>
<tr><td colspan="2">Assigned Technique: _____</td></tr>
<tr><td colspan="2">Assigned Repertoire: _____</td></tr>
<tr><td colspan="2">Practice session – amount of time: _____</td></tr>
<tr><td colspan="2">Goals for session: _____</td></tr>
<tr><td colspan="2">Practice strategies used: _____</td></tr>
<tr><td colspan="2">Self-evaluation: _____</td></tr>
</table>

**Figure 3.1. Practice Log**

## Build Self-Regulation into Ensemble Rehearsals

Beginning music learners in choral and instrumental ensembles must use self-regulation for success in performing groups such as middle and high school bands, orchestras, and choirs. Ensemble directors can teach beginners what it means to self-regulate during rehearsal. A poster on the wall with some questions regarding self-regulation might serve as a reminder. Figure 3.2 is an example of such a poster.

<u>**You Are In Charge of Your Music Learning!**</u>

**What will you do to get the most out of today's rehearsal?**

➢ **What is your GOAL to improve your musicianship, right here, right now, today?**

➢ **What STRATEGIES will you use for musical success today?**

➢ **At the end of rehearsal, will you honestly be able to tell yourself, "JOB WELL DONE"?**

➢ **In what ways will YOU make a positive contribution to the success of our ensemble today?**

**Figure 3.2. Self-Regulation Poster**

When planning instruction, teachers might remember that activities and assignments requiring students to self-regulate essentially "put the ball in their court" (to use a tennis analogy). Teachers can spoon-feed information and instructions to their students at all times, or teachers can provide necessary structure for students to take responsibility for their own learning. When teachers build self-regulation into instructional plans and assignments, they create a learning environment in which students are encouraged to develop autonomy as learners.

## NOTES

1. Susan Hallam, "Approaches to Instrumental Music Practice of Experts and Novices: Implications for Education," in *Does Practice Make Perfect? Current Theory and Research on Instrumental Music Practice*, edited by Harald Jørgensen and Andreas Lehmann (Oslo: Norges Musikkhøgskole, 1997), 93.

2. Emily Fox and Michelle Riconscente, "Metacognition and Self-Regulation in James, Piaget, and Vygotsky," *Educational Psychology Review* 20, no. 4 (2008): 374.

3. Barry J. Zimmerman, "Attaining Self-Regulation: A Social Cognitive Perspective," in *Handbook of Self-Regulation*, edited by Moske Zeidner, Paul R. Pintrich, and Monique Boekaerts (San Diego: Academic Press, 2000), 14.

4. Ibid.

5. Robert H. Woody, "Learning from the Experts: Applying Research in Expert Performance to Music Education," *Update: Applications of Research in Music Education* 19, no. 9 (2001): 11.

6. Betty T. Welsbacher and Elaine D. Bernstorf, "Musical Thinking among Diverse Students," in *Dimensions of Musical Learning and Teaching: A Different Kind of Classroom*, edited by Eunice Boardman (Reston, Va.: MENC, 2002), 158.

7. John H. Flavell, "Metacognition and Cognitive Monitoring: A New Area of Cognitive Developmental Inquiry," *American Psychologist* 34, no. 10 (1979): 910.

8. Zimmerman, "Attaining Self-Regulation," 34.

9. Fox and Riconscente, "Metacognition and Self-Regulation," 376–77; Barbara Z. Presseisen, *Thinking Skills: Research and Practice* (Washington, D.C.: National Education Association, 1986), 12–14; Robert J. Swartz and D. N. Perkins, *Teaching Thinking: Issues and Approaches* (Pacific Grove, Calif.: Midwest Publications, 1990), 178; Shawn Taylor, "Better Learning through

Better Thinking: Developing Students' Metacognitive Abilities," *Journal of College Reading and Learning* 30, no. 1 (1999): 42.

10. Presseisen, *Thinking Skills*, 11.

11. Gary E. McPherson and Barry J. Zimmerman, "Self-Regulation of Musical Learning: A Social Cognitive Perspective on Developing Performance Skills," in *MENC Handbook of Research on Music Learning, vol. 2: Applications*, edited by Richard Colwell and Peter R. Webster (New York: Oxford University Press, 2011), 132.

12. Peter Miksza, "The Development of a Measure of Self-Regulated Practice Behavior for Beginning and Intermediate Instrumental Music Students," *Journal of Research in Music Education* 59, no. 4 (2012): 322.

13. Douglas J. Hacker, "Definitions and Empirical Foundations," in *Metacognition in Educational Theory and Practice*, edited by Douglas J. Hacker, John Dunlosky, and Arthur C. Graesser (Mahwah, N.J.: Lawrence Erlbaum Associates, 1998), 16–17; Gregory Schraw, "Promoting General Metacognitive Awareness," in *Metacognition in Learning and Instruction: Theory, Research and Practice*, edited by Hope Hartman (Dordrecht, Netherlands: Kluwer Academic Publishers, 2001), 4.

14. Gregory Schraw, Kent J. Crippen, and Kendall Hartley, "Promoting Self-Regulation in Science Education: Metacognition as Part of a Broader Perspective on Learning," *Research in Science Education* 36 (2006): 114.

15. McPherson and Zimmerman, "Self-Regulation of Musical Learning," 158–62; Zimmerman, "Attaining Self-Regulation," 16–24.

16. Kacper Miklaszewski, "A Case Study of a Pianist Preparing a Musical Performance," *Psychology of Music* 17, no. 2 (1989): 95–109.

17. Siw G. Nielsen, "Self-Regulation of Learning Strategies during Practice: A Case Study of a Church Organ Student Preparing a Musical Work for Performance," in *Does Practice Make Perfect? Current Theory and Research on Instrumental Music Practice*, edited by Harald Jørgensen and Andreas Lehmann (Oslo: Norges Musikkhøgskole, 1997), 109.

18. Ibid., 110.

19. Ibid., 120.

20. Gary E. McPherson, "Cognitive Strategies and Skill Acquisition in Musical Performance," *Bulletin of the Council for Research in Music Education*, no. 133 (Summer 1997): 70.

21. Ibid.

22. Gary E. McPherson and James M. Renwick, "A Longitudinal Study of Self-Regulation in Children's Musical Practice," *Music Education Research* 3, no. 2 (2001): 170–71.

23. Ibid., 184.

24. Siw G. Nielsen, "Self-Regulating Learning Strategies in Instrumental Music Practice," *Music Education Research* 3, no. 2 (2001): 156.

25. Peter Miksza, "Relationships among Impulsiveness, Locus of Control, Sex, and Music Practice," *Journal of Research in Music Education* 54, no. 4 (2006): 320.

26. Ibid., 321.

27. James L. Byo and Jane W. Cassidy, "An Exploratory Study of Time Use in the Practice of Music Majors: Self-Report and Observation Analysis," *Update: Applications of Research in Music Education* 27, no. 1. (2008): 34.

28. Amanda Leon-Guerrero, "Self-Regulation Strategies Used by Student Musicians during Music Practice," *Music Education Research* 10, no. 1 (2008): 97.

29. Ibid., 91.

30. McPherson and Zimmerman, "Self-Regulation of Musical Learning," 134.

31. Miksza, "The Development of a Measure," 320.

32. Peter Miksza, Stephanie Prichard, and Diana Sorbo, "An Observational Study of Intermediate Band Students' Self-Regulated Practice Behaviors," *Journal of Research in Music Education* 60, no. 3 (2012): 255.

33. Ibid., 263.

34. Flavell, "Metacognition and Cognitive Monitoring," 909–10.

35. Bernadette de Jager, Margo Jansen, and Gerry Reezigt, "The Development of Metacognition in Primary School Learning Environments," *School Effectiveness and School Improvement* 16, no. 2 (2005): 180–81.

36. Arthur L. Costa and Lawrence F. Lowery, *Techniques for Teaching Thinking* (Pacific Grove, Calif.: Midwest Publications, 1989), 64.

37. Lyle Davidson and Larry Scripp, "Education and Development in Music from a Cognitive Perspective," in *Children and the Arts*, edited by David J. Hargreaves (Philadelphia: Open University Press, 1989), 61.

**4**

# METACOGNITION AND SELF-REFLECTION FOR MUSIC LEARNING

*S*elf-reflection, *reflecting on learning*, and *reflective thinking* are interchangeable terms for an important component of metacognition. Metacognition involves being aware of what one knows or does not know and is used by learners for memory retrieval.[1] It is the process of self-reflection that makes this possible. When learners engage in metacognitive self-reflection, they revisit a learning experience to make note of how the process unfolded. Self-reflective learners acknowledge mistakes and remember important points in their learning experiences; and they make connections among past learning experiences, current learning experiences, and possibilities for future learning. This type of reflective thinking distinguishes active learning from passive learning.[2] Jack Lochhead asserted the imperative for reflective thinking when he asserted that "reflective thinking is essential to metacognition, the process of thinking about thinking. We can understand another person's thinking only to the extent that we can model it with our own thinking. Thus, as long as our own thoughts remain opaque, the thoughts of others are even more obscure. Without reflective thinking we remain lost in a mental fog that we cannot see and have no reason to believe exists. Therefore until we can think reflectively, we have no idea what we have been missing."[3]

## SEQUENTIAL STEPS IN LEARNERS' SELF-REFLECTIONS

Self-reflection may be understood as a linear process that unfolds in the minds of metacognitive learners during and following any learning experiences. Kerka delineated five steps in self-reflection for learning.[4] The first step is *descriptive*, in which the learner acknowledges that a learning task has been completed. The next step is *metacognitive*, in which the learner examines the thought processes that were used to complete the learning task. Following this, the learner engages in *analysis* of events involved in the learning task, considering what happened and *why* it happened. Next, the learner *evaluates* the outcomes of the learning task. In the fifth and final *reconstructive* step, the learner considers whether and how the learning task can be successfully completed in the future. It is through these five steps that a learner is able to construct real learning from self-reflection in a learning experience.[5]

Generally speaking, students would not engage in all five of the self-reflective steps without being prompted by their teacher. The following writing prompts for music learning might help students to move through the self-reflection process toward a meaningful conclusion.

### Writing Prompts for Music Learning

1. *The descriptive step.* "This is the music-learning event . . ."
2. *The metacognitive step.* "These are the thought processes that made music learning possible for me . . ."
3. *The analysis step.* "These are the things that happened during the music-learning event . . ."
4. *The evaluation step.* "This is the outcome of the music learning . . ."
5. *The reconstructive step.* "This is how I will make future music-learning events even better . . ."

The music teacher would want to substitute appropriate, specific terms for *music-learning event*, such as "concert," "rehearsal," "festival performance," or "band trip," as needed.

If their teacher outlines the steps and provides writing prompts, it is possible for students to move quickly through the five steps, even in a short self-reflective journal entry. To clarify, let us consider the following scenario in which high school choral-music students might progress through the five steps in self-reflection for learning.

1. Following a choral concert, the director asks students to write in their journals a brief description of the concert experience (the *descriptive* step).
2. Next, the choral director asks students to write a recollection of the thought processes that they used while learning and rehearsing the pieces for performance (the *metacognitive* step).
3. After the students examine their personal thought processes, the director asks them to write about how the choir performed, including *why* and *how* certain things happened during performance (the *analysis* step).
4. Next, the choral director asks students to write brief self-evaluations of their own parts in the choral performance and of the ensemble as a whole (the *evaluation* step).
5. Finally, the director asks students to bring the reflective-writing process to a close by making suggestions about how they can work on specific skills to improve future choral performances (the *reconstructive* step).

By providing class time and writing prompts for a journaling activity such as this, the music teacher allows students to bring closure to the

**Photo 4.1.   Middle School Choir**

period of time in which they worked toward the common goal of a concert performance. Additionally, the teacher encourages students to assign their own meanings to the experience and to begin thinking about a new period of preparation for the next performance.

## ENCOURAGING SELF-REFLECTION FOR MUSIC LEARNING

Music learning involves action and understanding, skill development and applied knowledge. Young musicians progress from a point of *inability* to play or sing, improvise, compose, and listen deeply and intelligently to a point of *ability* to do these things, in capacities relevant to their ages and levels of advancement. Along the way, music learners encounter new information, challenges, difficulties, and triumphs. The habit of thinking reflectively about their musical experiences allows learners to absorb, or internalize, all that is new and strange in order to make it their own, thereby enabling future progress. Self-reflection enriches learners' experiences in that they become aware of themselves as musicians. According to Leon-Guerrero, reflective thinking is the "foundation for what is now referred to as an executive process of metacognition, *self-regulated* thinking," among students engaged in music learning.[6]

Music educators help their students when they place emphasis on self-reflection, as it is a crucial aspect of developing a musician's sense of self-awareness regarding artistic processes, strengths, and weaknesses. Self-reflection enables music learners to become self-directed[7] and to engage in self-assessment.[8] Hence, reflective thinking is often associated with concepts of critical thinking or higher-order thinking.[9]

In an examination of music development from a cognitive point of view, Davidson and Scripp posited that reflective thinking in music begins in adolescence and is typically observed in learners who have some musical training. According to them, "cognitive psychologists refer to the more advanced levels in terms of reflective thinking. The reflective musician is more apt to demonstrate declarative knowledge (concepts that stand for events, strings of events, or abstractions) or procedural knowledge (analysis or descriptions about how things are accomplished). These form the basis for reflective thinking about music."[10]

There is nothing new about the idea of encouraging learners to enrich their educational experiences through self-reflection. In 1933, John

---

**Tips for Teachers**

At the beginning of a school year, require each student to bring a spiral notebook to music class. Provide a shelf, crate, or cubby for each class to keep their notebooks in the music classroom. Use the notebooks throughout the year for students to write reflective journals, listening logs, or practice logs.

---

Dewey defined reflective thinking as follows: "*Reflective* thinking, in distinction from other operations to which we apply the name of thought, involves (1) a state of doubt, hesitation, perplexity, mental difficulty, in which thinking originates and (2) an act of searching, hunting, inquiring, to find material that will resolve the doubt, settle and dispose of the perplexity."[11] It was Dewey's opinion that teachers have a responsibility to serve as guides for learning by setting up opportunities for learners to exercise curiosity and make connections that lead to reflective thought. Dewey believed that "we do have to learn *how* to think well, especially *how* to acquire the general *habit* of reflecting."[12]

Although Dewey's definition of reflective thinking appears to center on problem solving, Richardson and Whitaker proposed that reflective thinking in music need not have, as its object, a problem to be solved. Instead, they stated that reflective thinking in music might include emotion and imagination. To think reflectively in music, learners might access their memories of previous music making or listening experiences.[13] As such, reflective thinking in music encompasses the affective-learning domain as well as the cognitive domain.

## OVERVIEW OF RESEARCH ON SELF-REFLECTION IN MUSIC EDUCATION

### 1990—In an Investigative Study, Davidson and Scripp Introduced the "Ensemble Critique" for High School Band Students.

In association with Harvard Project Zero, researchers Davidson and Scripp implemented a study of reflective thinking among students in instrumental-music ensembles.[14] Their method was to develop an Ensemble Critique Form, show students how to use it, and provide time in rehearsals for students to use the critique for reflecting on their personal progress as well as progress of the ensemble. Davidson and Scripp found that self-reflection allowed students to develop awareness of themselves as musicians.

The researchers asserted that production (playing, performing music) should not be the total focus of learning in a performing ensemble but that perception and reflection are equally important for "significant learning."[15] More information on this study is presented in chapter 5, Metacognition and Self-Evaluation for Music Learning.

## 2002 and 2005—Hewitt Acknowledged the Inter-Relatedness of Self-Reflection and Self-Evaluation for Music Learning.

Hewitt published two experimental studies of self-evaluation processes among students in middle school and high school instrumental ensembles. In both studies, Hewitt noted that self-reflection is the final phase of self-regulation and that self-reflection consists of the following: (1) self-judgment (self-evaluation and causal attribution) and (2) self-reaction (self-satisfaction/affect and adaptive defense).[16] Hewitt's studies are summarized more completely in the following chapter.

## 2008—In An Investigative Study, Band Students Developed Greater Autonomy in Rehearsals Through Self-Reflection.

While working with middle school band students, Bauer used the ensemble-critique form developed by Arts Propel project researchers Davidson and Scripp. Bauer's method included having students discuss and write reflections after playing a piece or after listening to a recording of themselves playing a piece. Bauer implemented his study among a group of 106 middle school band members over a period of six weeks. Students used the Ensemble Critique Form once each week. They were asked to evaluate their own performances and that of the ensemble and to write reflectively about their own playing and that of the group.

As a result, students did appear to significantly improve their ability to diagnose and solve performance problems, and student practice time significantly increased. The increased practice time may have been a result of emphasis placed on strategies (a component of metacognition) during class time. Gaining knowledge of practice strategies may have been the factor that sparked students' increased interest in individual practice.[17] The subject of practice strategies is covered more completely in chapter 7.

## 2011—In An Experimental Study, Children in General-Music Classes Demonstrated Critical-Thinking Skills in Reflective Writings about Music-Listening Experiences.

The ability to reflect on learning is a component of metacognition and critical thinking. At the same time, learners who are instructed in critical thinking develop a greater ability to engage in self-reflection.

Daniel Johnson implemented a study among fifth-grade students in general-music classes, investigating the effects of instruction in critical thinking on learners' development of listening skills, as measured by written reflections on listening experiences. Johnson believed that reflection is inherent in the constructivist approach to music teaching, with its emphasis on learners constructing meaning from their musical experiences. He found that critical-thinking instruction had a "significant and positive effect on participants' music-listening responses," noting that learners who received critical-thinking instruction (in the study) wrote reflections that "demonstrated enhanced depth and greater detail" as compared with reflections written by students who did not receive instruction in critical thinking.[18] Results of Johnson's study substantiated the claim that metacognitive skills can be taught and that, once taught, they have an enriching effect on music learners' experiences.

## 2011—Researchers Included Self-Reflection in a New Seven-Step Strategy for Creative-Music Teaching.

The *creative-music strategy* is an instructional model developed by Robinson, Bell, and Pogonowski. According to the researchers, it is "a dynamic and flexible seven-step model for guiding general-music students through the music concepts of improvisation and composition, followed by critical reflection."[19]

Robinson, Bell, and Pogonowki advocated that music teachers should stimulate thinking among their students by asking open-ended questions where there are no right or wrong answers but, instead, a number of possible options: "When students believe that their thinking is valued and respected by their community of peers and teacher, their confidence to share their musical thoughts increases and happens more freely, fluidly, and frequently."[20] Step seven in the creative-music strategy is "reflective analysis." This final step of self-reflection is important because it helps learners to develop critical-thinking skills and serves as a springboard for their next round of creativity.[21]

## JOURNALING: AN INSTRUCTIONAL STRATEGY FOR SELF-REFLECTION

A review of the literature on metacognitive self-reflection in education yields many examples of educators using journal writing as a classroom activity to enrich learning and promote critical thinking among students. Barell, Liebmann, and Sigel suggested that teachers should require students to keep thinking journals in which they write reflectively about their thinking processes related to schoolwork.[22] The authors provided questions to guide students in their reflective writing. A sample of these questions includes asking, "What was the problem I had to solve? How did I solve it? (Identify thinking strategies, not solutions). Did I solve it? Well? What would I do differently next time? Why? What did I learn about my problem-solving abilities?"[23] Keeping a journal helps learners to become more self-aware regarding their own thinking processes and allows them to set goals and devise their own strategies for learning.

Writing in a personal journal or log helps learners to synthesize an experience[24]; however, teachers may use flexibility in defining what constitutes a journal. Students may write traditional journal entries, but they may also illustrate their written journals, or they might develop series of video or audio recordings that collectively become reflective-learning journals.[25] Video or audio journals would be particularly appropriate in music classes.

## SUGGESTIONS FOR SELF-REFLECTIVE JOURNALING IN MUSIC LEARNING

The following list details some ideas for journal-writing activities in various settings where music learning takes place.

### Reflections on Daily Activities in General-Music Classes

Music teachers can encourage students to reflect on their musical progress, on new learning, on challenges and difficulties, on composition projects, or on a host of other typical learning activities in music classes. General-music teachers might require students to supply spiral notebooks for music class. These can be kept in the music classroom, and teachers can provide some time for journal writing on a daily or weekly basis.

It is helpful for music teachers to provide writing prompts that stimulate students' self-reflection. These are most often presented in the form of unfinished sentences that students are encouraged to finish and expand on. The following is a list of suggested writing prompts for self-reflective learning journals in general-music classes.

"Today in music class, we learned . . ."
"My biggest challenge in music learning is . . ."
"I am most happy in music class when . . ."
"My best musical achievement is . . ."
"In music class, I am getting better at . . ."
"Since the beginning of the school year, I have learned . . ."
"My musical composition is . . ."
"The next part of my musical composition will be . . ."
"My favorite musical instrument is _____ because . . ."
"My favorite song is _____ because . . ."
"My favorite composer is _____ because . . ."
"I know that I am a musician because I can . . ."
"The hardest thing to do in music is _____ because . . ."
"Music is important because . . ."

## Listening Logs

Music teachers might play a recording of a different piece of music each day or each week and encourage students to write self-reflective journal entries regarding their listening experiences. In addition to noting titles, composers, and other identifying information about a piece, music teachers can encourage students to reflect on their own responses to the music and to write about them descriptively. Figure 4.1 shows a template for a self-reflective entry in a listening log.

---

**Listening Log**

Name _____ Date _____

Title of piece: _____

Composer: _____

Date and period of composition: _____

Information about composition: _____

_____

My personal reflection on listening: *How do you feel when listening to this piece? What do you think about when listening to this piece? Why? Explain.*

_____

_____

_____

_____

_____

---

**Figure 4.1.  Listening Log**

## Self-Reflection in Secondary Music-Performance Ensembles

Directors of bands, choirs, and orchestras in middle schools and high schools typically provide ample opportunities for students to acquire musical knowledge, develop performance skills, and apply knowledge and skills in challenging and rewarding public performances and contests. The time requirements for running a successful band, choir, or orchestra program are so great that many directors do not take the time to incorporate journal writing into their rehearsals. But researchers (referenced earlier in this chapter) indicate that there are real rewards for encouraging self-reflective writing in performing ensembles. To encourage metacognitive self-reflection regarding developing musicianship, directors might provide writing prompts that require students to think about their thought processes related to performing in the ensemble. Some suggested writing prompts follow.

"My greatest strength in playing/singing is . . ."
"My greatest challenge in playing/singing is . . ."
"I can plan for effective learning in band/choir/orchestra by doing this . . ."
"I can monitor my progress in band/choir/orchestra by doing this . . ."
"The musical skill that I am currently working on is . . ."
"My strategies for working on musical skills are . . ."
"In today's rehearsal, my greatest strength was . . ."
"In today's rehearsal, my greatest weakness was . . ."
"My strategy for overall excellence in band/choir/orchestra is . . ."
"My best memory from band/choir/orchestra this year is . . ."
"I can make a contribution to my band/choir/orchestra by doing this . . ."
"I am preparing for our next concert by doing this . . ."
"I contributed to a successful band/choir/orchestra concert by doing this . . ."
"Being in band/choir/orchestra means this to me . . ."

Writing prompts, such as those listed above, are effective when students write free-form self-reflections in notebook journals. Another approach is for directors to print out templates for students to write journal entries on a weekly basis. Figure 4.2 shows a template for weekly self-reflection by students in a middle or high school band, choir, or orchestra.

**<u>Self-Reflection for Band/Choir/Orchestra Members</u>**

Name: _____ .Week of _____ - _____

My current strengths in band/choir/orchestra are:

_____
_____
_____

My current weaknesses in band/choir/orchestra are:

_____
_____
_____

My current strategies for meeting challenges in band/choir/orchestra are:

_____
_____
_____

My current general feelings about band/choir/orchestra are:

_____
_____
_____

**Figure 4.2. Band/Choir/Orchestra Self-Reflection**

## Self-Reflection on Special Musical Experiences

Music education involves a natural ebb and flow related to the fact that music is a performing art. Students and directors in performing ensembles engage in cycles of learning, rehearsing, and performing. When one concert, festival, or show is completed, it is time to begin preparations for the next performance. The process of self-reflection allows students in performing ensembles to collect their thoughts and assign meaning to a performance event before moving on to preparations for the next event.

Similarly, students in nonperforming general-music classes sometimes experience live performances or music lecture-demonstrations. These might be presented by visiting artists or teachers, or students

**Photo 4.2. High School Band, Percussion**

might take field trips to attend concerts. Music teachers can help students to create enriched learning outcomes from these experiences by providing time for them to write self-reflective journal entries following special music events. Some suggested writing prompts follow.

"My favorite part of the symphony concert was . . ."
"I learned this from the percussion demonstration . . ."
"I am a better musician after our choir tour because . . ."
"Listening to the band concert made me feel . . ."
"When our class went to the opera, I learned . . ."
"I will never forget our spring concert because . . ."
"Before our festival performance, I was . . . but now I am . . ."

## QUESTIONING AND CLASS DISCUSSION: AN INSTRUCTIONAL STRATEGY FOR SELF-REFLECTION

Journal writing is probably the most common format for self-reflection, but it takes time and at least some minimal supplies of pencils and either paper or notebooks, plus writing prompts provided by the teacher. To

save time and integrate reflection into ongoing music activities, teachers can encourage students to self-reflect by way of verbal reports in
classroom discussions. A knowledgeable teacher can guide discussions
through carefully phrased questions to stimulate metacognitive self-
reflection among students.

The important thing for teachers to remember is that questions
should prompt students to explore their own thinking and learning processes. Therefore, rather than simply focusing on content knowledge,
teachers might question students regarding *how* they think about their
learning and music making. When teachers ask open-ended questions to
stimulate class discussion, students might be inspired to share metacognitive self-reflection with their peers. As metacognitive sharing unfolds,
students begin to learn from each other as well as from their teacher.

While investigating the effects of self-reflection among students in
math classes, Cobb, Boufi, McClain, and Whitenack found beneficial
effects when teachers guided students to reflect on their thinking during classroom discussions.[26] The topic of reflective classroom discussions
was not specific answers to math problems but, rather, the mathematical processes used by students to work the problems. Because students
were encouraged to think about their own thought processes and to
share them with the class, they used metacognition. The researchers
concluded that classroom discourse "supports and enables" students'
reflections on learning, leading to positive learning outcomes.[27]

Like the math teachers in Cobb's study, music teachers might use
questioning techniques and classroom discussion to encourage self-
reflective thinking among music students. Some examples of questions
requiring self-reflection in music classes follow.

1. *Questions for a basic music theory class.* When constructing triads,
   how can you be sure that you are correct? What is your strategy for
   determining if a triad is major, minor, diminished, or augmented?
   How do you know? Can you devise a strategy for checking your
   answers before handing in an assignment? Describe your strategy.
   When (under what circumstances) do you apply your strategy?
2. *Questions for a performing ensemble.* What will you do to express
   the composer's intent in this section of the piece? What will you
   think about when we get to this climactic point to help you play/

sing expressively? What will you listen for in the band/choir at this point in the music? Can you describe how your part fits into the whole fabric of the music at this point? What will you think in order to ensure that your own playing/singing is most effective at this point in the music?

3. *Questions for a one-to-one instrumental lesson.* How will you practice this passage of music in order to make it clean and steady at a fast tempo? What are your practice strategies for a passage such as this? Can you describe the strategies that you will use in at-home practice to get this passage up to tempo without errors by next lesson? What will you do if you run into difficulties while you are practicing independently? How do you figure out problems for yourself when practicing at home?

4. *Questions for a general-music class.* How do you recognize time-value names of notes? What is your strategy for deciding if a note is a quarter, eighth, or half note? How do you know? What do you do when you listen to music in a focused way? Can you describe what you are thinking when you listen deeply to music? What activity helps you most to concentrate on listening to music? Describe your strategy for creating an ostinato. What do you listen for? How can you know if your ostinato will fit with the song?

5. *Questions for a music-appreciation class.* Describe your thought processes when listening to a new piece of music. What do you listen for? Describe your personal response to Baroque-period music as compared with your response to contemporary music. In what ways do you respond to these two different styles of music? Why? What causes you to respond to these two styles in different ways? Describe a strategy that you use to determine the style period of a piece when you are hearing it for the first time.

Music educators reading this chapter might quickly compose many more questions to stimulate self-reflection among students in various music-learning situations. The basic premise is to construct questions in such a way that students do not simply respond with factual bits of information they might have learned by rote but, rather, share their thought processes and help each other learn to solve musical problems for themselves. The benefit of metacognitive self-reflection in class discussions, as compared with journal writing, is that metacognition becomes socially shared among students. The topic of socially shared metacognition will be explored more fully in chapter 6, Socially Shared Metacognition: Thinking Aloud for Music Learning.

## NOTES

1. Janet Metcalfe and Hedy Kober, "Self-Reflective Consciousness and the Projectable Self," in *The Missing Link in Cognition: Origins of Self-Reflective Consciousness*, edited by Herbert S. Terrace and Janet Metcalfe (New York: Oxford University Press, 2005), 73.

2. Petros Georghiades, "From the General to the Situated: Three Decades of Metacognition," *International Journal of Science Education* 26, no. 3 (2004): 371.

3. Jack Lochhead, "Sound Thinking with Thinkback 2000" (paper presented at the Technological Education and National Development Conference, "Crossroads of the Millennium," April 8–10, 2000, Abu Dhabi, United Arab Emirates), 10.

4. Sandra Kerka, "Journal Writing as an Adult Learning Tool: Practice Application Brief No. 22," sponsored by the Office of Educational Research and Improvement (ED) (Columbus, Ohio: ERIC Clearing House on Adult, Career, and Vocational Education, 2002), http://files.eric.ed.gov/fulltext/ED470782.pdf, cited in Annaliese Homan, *Constructing Knowledge through Reflection* (Phoenix: League for Innovation in the Community College, 2006), 21–22.

5. Homan, *Constructing Knowledge*, 22.

6. Amanda Leon-Guerrero, "Self-Regulation Strategies Used by Student Musicians during Music Practice," *Music Education Research* 10, no. 1 (2008): 92.

7. John Barell, Rosemarie Liebmann, and Irving Sigel, "Fostering Thoughtful Self-Direction in Students," *Educational Leadership* 45, no. 7 (1988): 15–16.

8. Lyle Davidson and Larry Scripp, "Tracing Reflective Thinking in the Performance Ensemble," *Quarterly Journal of Music Teaching and Learning* 1, no. 1 (1990): 51.

9. Carol P. Richardson and Nancy L. Whitaker, "Critical Thinking and Music Education," in *Handbook of Research on Music Teaching and Learning*, edited by Richard Colwell (New York: Schirmer Books, 1992), 546.

10. Lyle Davidson and Larry Scripp, "Education and Development in Music from a Cognitive Perspective," in *Children and the Arts*, edited by David J. Hargreaves (Philadelphia: Open University Press, 1989), 79.

11. John Dewey, *How We Think: A Restatement of the Relation of Reflective Thinking to the Educative Process* (New York: D. C. Heath and Company, 1933), 12.

12. Ibid., 35.

13. Richardson and Whitaker, "Critical Thinking," 556.

14. Davidson and Scripp, "Tracing Reflective Thinking," 52.

15. Ibid., 51.

16. Michael P. Hewitt, "Self-Evaluation Accuracy among High School and Middle School Instrumentalists," *Journal of Research in Music Education* 53, no. 2 (2005): 149; Michael P. Hewitt, "Self-Evaluation Tendencies of Junior High Instrumentalists," *Journal of Research in Music Education* 50, no. 3 (2002): 216.

17. William I. Bauer, "Metacognition and Middle School Band Students," *Journal of Band Research* 43, no. 2 (2008): 50–63.

18. Daniel Johnson, "The Effect of Critical Thinking Instruction on Verbal Descriptions of Music," *Journal of Research in Music Education* 59, no. 3 (2011): 266.

19. Nathalie G. Robinson, Cindy L. Bell, and Lenore Pogonowski, "The Creative Music Strategy," *Music Educators Journal* 97, no. 3 (2011): 50–51.

20. Ibid., 52.

21. Ibid., 54–55.

22. Barrell, Liebmann, and Sigel, "Fostering Thoughtful Self-Direction," 14.

23. Ibid., 15.

24. Susan Farrell, *Tools for Powerful Student Evaluation* (Ft. Lauderdale, Fla.: Meredith Music Publications, 1997), 20.

25. Arthur L. Costa and Lawrence F. Lowery, *Techniques for Teaching Thinking* (Pacific Grove, Calif.: Midwest Publications, 1989), 72.

26. Paul Cobb, Ada Boufi, Kay McClain, and Joy Whitenack, "Reflective Discourse and Collective Reflection," *Journal for Research in Mathematics Education* 28, no. 3 (1997): 258–59, 274.

27. Ibid., 266.

# 5

# METACOGNITION AND SELF-EVALUATION IN MUSIC LEARNING

Teachers routinely evaluate the products of student learning on an ongoing basis. Whether evaluation is formal or informal, teachers use it to give feedback to students and to inform planning for instruction. Music teachers evaluate students' progress in continuous, minute-to-minute analyses of students' performances in classes, rehearsals, and individual lessons. Evaluation is embedded in the fabric of reciprocal processes that characterize ongoing interactions between music teachers and learners. Metacognitive learners develop the ability to evaluate themselves rather than being solely dependent on feedback from teachers. As music students increasingly engage in self-evaluation, they might become more independent learners.

As stated in chapter 1, numerous educational researchers define primary metacognitive skills as (1) planning, (2) self-monitoring, and (3) self-evaluating, and they observe that metacognitive learners engage in these actions before, during, and after engaging in learning tasks. In chapter 4 we considered the apparent effects of self-reflection on music learning, as well as instructional strategies designed to promote self-reflection among music learners. Self-reflection leads naturally to self-evaluation (sometimes called *self-assessment*). Whereas self-reflection may or may not involve judgment on the part of the student, the nature of self-evaluation implies some level of judgment regarding the relative success of the student's learning outcomes.

While engaging in self-evaluation, learners judge their work against preexisting standards or criteria, generally imposed by the teacher or some other exemplary model. For this reason, self-evaluation tends to be more structured than self-reflection. Nevertheless, self-evaluation enjoys the same relationship with metacognition as self-reflection does: it is an action that requires metacognition, and, at the same time, it is a component of metacognition.

Educational researchers have investigated students' self-evaluations in academic subject areas. For example, in an action-research project conducted among children in grades K through 5, the team of Cunningham, Krull, Land, and Russell implemented a program where students engaged in goal setting and self-evaluation. At the outset of the study, researchers were concerned with students' apparent lack of metacognitive skills.[1] Through a program of increased emphasis on goal setting and self-evaluation activities, the children showed improvements in four areas: (1) persistence, (2) problem solving, (3) motivation, and (4) accuracy.[2]

Student self-evaluation leads to increased metacognition and self-regulation when teachers encourage learners to think about their own thought processes related to learning tasks. Therefore, teachers might encourage students to self-evaluate not only whether they "got it right" but also how they went about completing a learning task. It is not enough for students to get the right answer with little or no deep understanding. Teachers who promote metacognitive self-evaluation help their students to focus on thinking and learning processes, thereby setting the stage for greater student autonomy that leads to independent, lifelong learning.[3]

Self-evaluation is beneficial for students in music classes, as well as in regular academic-learning environments. Hale and Green asserted that self-assessment leads to autonomy for lifelong learning among music students. They stated the following conclusions:

> In our experience, fostering the ability of students to assess themselves is one of the ultimate goals of instruction. As instructors, we must teach students to function autonomously when they leave school and no longer have our guidance. Helping students learn to self-assess teaches them

to look beyond their own point of view and see themselves in relation to a standard. It also teaches empowerment. As students eventually understand and internalize the standard, they will not be as dependent on authorities to make corrections or judgments concerning their work. They will be able to use standards and goals themselves to continue improving.[4]

Educators generally think of self-evaluation as coming *after* a learning task is completed. But self-evaluation is also beneficial for students *during* a learning task, especially if the task is extended over a period of time, such as when music students prepare repertoire for performance or work on music-composition projects. Self-testing and reflection are two student activities that lead to metacognitive self-knowledge and result in self-regulation. Therefore, it is helpful when teachers embed self-evaluation activities into the procedures for students' learning tasks.[5]

Students can measure the degree to which their learning outcomes are successful against criteria imposed by the teacher. Or they can self-evaluate based on personal goals that they set at the beginning of a project or learning task. Either way, it is important for students to take this personal responsibility, although it is generally within the provenance of the music teacher to make a final evaluation or give a grade. For this reason, student self-evaluations are generally used as formative assessments rather than summative assessments. The teacher holds final authority for grading; however, if lifelong learning is a goal of music education, then the process of students learning to self-evaluate is as important as any final grade.

---

### Tips for Teachers

Students in high school bands, choirs, and orchestras can record individual performance tests at regular intervals throughout a school year. Sound files can be kept on students' flash drives, and students can listen to these recordings for self-evaluation purposes. Teachers might provide rubrics on which students write self-evaluations according to lists of performance criteria. At the end of the school year, students can review their recorded tests and their self-evaluation rubrics. This process allows students to engage in summative reflection on progress made throughout the year.

## OVERVIEW OF RESEARCH ON SELF-EVALUATION IN MUSIC LEARNING

Several music education researchers have investigated aspects of student self-evaluation and have found varying results. Most notably, researchers have explored instructional practices such as providing a recorded model, providing teacher-guided structure, and having students listen to video- or audio-recorded examples of their own performances.

### 1990—High School Band Students Became More "Self-Directed"[6] When They Were Trained to Self-Evaluate Specific Elements of Ensemble Performance.

Chapter 4 referenced the self-reflective nature of student activities included in the investigative study conducted by Davidson and Scripp. Here we will focus on the student self-evaluation activities devised by the researchers. In the study, band directors taught students how to use the Ensemble Critique Form and allowed time in rehearsals for students to complete the forms. The ongoing self-reflective activity included self-evaluation based on specific criteria. Preparations included defining musical terms and discussing important musical issues on which students should focus. Details provided on the critique form included a list of musical "dimensions" for consideration, as follows: "rhythm, intonation, tone, balance, articulation, phrasing, interpretation, etc., or any dimension specified by the teacher."[7] Students were asked to specify dimensions and measure numbers in the music as they wrote self-evaluative comments regarding their own instrumental sections (immediately after performance) and the whole ensemble (after listening to a recording of group performance). An important next step required students to write suggestions for strategies to correct errors or improve musical dimensions for their sections and for the whole ensemble.

After implementing the ensemble-rehearsal critique in rehearsals over a period of several weeks, band directors in Davidson and Scripp's study began to see changes in the interpersonal dynamics of their ensembles. Student thinking became more visible as directors were able to read the written self-evaluations and suggestions from students. Students began to view music scores and rehearsals from the perspective of the composer or director. A not-always-welcomed by-product was that students sometimes challenged the authority of the director or composer in musical decisions. Because of time spent in reflection and self-evaluation, students became more self-directive. These changes culminated in a shift in the director-student relationship to be more interactive and less autocratic. Regarding this new relationship, Davidson and Scripp observed that "reflective thinking serves both ends of the relationship. On the one hand, students need advice on how to think about their music and related performance problems. On the other hand, by knowing how the student formulates musical concepts and seeks to transform performance problems, the director knows what level of advice to offer."[8]

## 1993—In an Exploratory Study, Music Students' Self-Evaluations Were Not in Agreement with Evaluations Given by Their Peers and Music-Faculty Members.

In a study of peer evaluation and self-evaluation among collegiate brass players, Martin Bergee found that student self-evaluations correlated poorly with both peer evaluations and faculty evaluations of students. He stated that "self-evaluation requires focus and structure. Specific behaviors must be targeted and carefully defined, and assessment instruments must draw students' attention to positive as well as to negative aspects."[9] Bergee concluded that in order for collegiate players to make meaningful, productive self-evaluations, they might benefit from structure and guidance provided by faculty members.[10] If this is true for college music majors, then K-through-12 music educators might assume that their students will need even more focus and structure to acquire skill in self-evaluation.

## 1995—In An Experimental Study, Middle School Band Students Engaged in Self-Evaluation of Music Performance.

In a study of the effects of self-evaluation on music performance, motivation, and self-esteem among middle school instrumentalists, Randall Aitchison reached similar conclusions to those of Bergee regarding the need for teachers to provide guidance and structure for students' self-evaluations. Aitchison studied self-evaluation among seventh- and eighth-grade band students, using four modes, as follows: (1) teacher-only evaluation (with no student involvement), (2) teacher-driven self-evaluation (with student involvement), (3) student-driven self-evaluation (with teacher involvement), and (4) student-only self-evaluation (with no teacher involvement).[11] He found that student-only self-evaluation (unaided by teacher guidance) was not beneficial to students. According to Aitchison, "the lack of teacher guidance in the focusing of critical reflection likely hindered the ability of students to identify musical problems and self-administer appropriate diagnostic feedback."[12] Results showed that although teacher-only evaluation appeared to have immediate positive effects as students worked to correct errors pointed out by their director, the effects may not have lasted over time. It appeared that when students did not engage in any self-evaluation, they were less willing to maintain motivation for working on music tasks over time. Aitchison found that, when given a choice, middle school band students preferred to have evaluation shared between teacher and students, involving some degree of student self-evaluation with teacher guidance and input.[13]

## 1997—In An Investigative Study, College Piano Students Self-Evaluated, Using Five Established Criteria, as Follows: (1) Hand Position, (2) Correct Fingering, (3) Technique, (4) Sight-Reading, and (5) Musicality.[14]

Marilyn Kostka compared student self-evaluations with teacher evaluations of college piano students and found results similar to those found by Bergee and Aitchison. Results showed only a low to moderate degree of agreement between student self-evaluations and teacher evaluations of student performances.[15] Like Bergee and Aitchison, Kostka concluded that students needed structure and teacher guidance to make meaningful self-evaluations. "If keyboard students were taught to perform self-assessment based on operationally defined skills, such as the five in this investigation, the result might be more objective, positive, and productive self-evaluations, provided that students understood the purpose of the evaluations."[16]

## 2001—In An Experimental Study, Junior High School Band Students Who Self-Evaluated in Reference to an Exemplary Model Were Able to Improve Their Playing.

In a study of self-evaluation among instrumentalists, Michael Hewitt found that it is beneficial to provide a model recording against which students can self-evaluate their playing. Students who self-evaluated after listening to a model recording were able to achieve higher scores in performance tests for technique, rhythmic accuracy, interpretation, and overall performance. The same beneficial effects were not achieved by students who listened to the exemplary model but did not engage in self-evaluation. Hewitt concluded that music teachers should encourage students to use recorded models as standards for self-evaluation.[17]

## 2001—Music Students at An Australian University Used Metacognitive Skills to Engage in Self-Evaluations of Music Performances.

Ryan Daniel reported on a new approach to performance evaluation. Students' performances were routinely videotaped in concert practice classes. Immediately following the classes, students were required to view their videotapes, and each student was required to write a three hundred–word self-critical reflection. University music teachers provide the following outline for self-evaluations:

1. *Personal presentation.* Entrance and exit, bowing, physical presence, characteristic mannerisms, etc.
2. *Musical issues.* Accuracy, stylistic appropriateness, choice of repertoire.
3. *Overall impression.* Personal response, audience response.
4. *Reflections on actual performance* via viewing the video as against perceived performance.
5. *Reflections on progress.* Improvements and developments since previous performance.
6. *Directions.* Plans to improve and enhance performance.[18]

Metacognitive skills were required of students as they followed the outline for writing critical self-reflections regarding achievement of musical goals, improvements and developments over time, and plans to improve performance. The metacognitive skills of planning, monitoring, and evaluating were clearly evident in the critical-reflection outline that was used in Daniel's study. Results showed that 80 percent of students felt the process of writing critical self-reflections did contribute to enhanced performance skills. And when questioned regarding the value of using videotapes as a basis for critical self-reflection, 57 percent of the students responded that the process was "highly valuable," 26 percent responded that the process was "moderately valuable," and 11 percent responded that the process was "somewhat valuable."[19]

Daniel concluded that the practice of videotaping students' music performances and requiring students to write self-evaluative reflections was beneficial for music students. The videotapes and written self-evaluations provided documentation of progress over time. Additionally, Daniel predicted other far-reaching benefits, as follows: "The writing of reports also serves to develop critical skills that are essential to any student interested in pedagogy at various levels. With regard to performance, the process serves to further develop students' self-reflective skills that, once they have graduated, are crucial to their career prospects in the profession."[20]

## 2002—In An Investigative Study Among College Instrumentalists, the Sharing of Inflated Peer Evaluations May Have Led to Inflated Self-Evaluations.[21]

Bergee and Cecconi-Roberts found that avoiding teacher involvement in the self-evaluation process might prevent students from reaping benefits of music-performance self-evaluation.[22] They suggested that teacher involvement is necessary to guide students in self-evaluation, particularly in beginning stages. Additionally, the researchers did not find strong agreement between self-evaluation and evaluation provided by others (teachers or peers). They further recommended that peer evaluation should be used judiciously, due to finding that students are easily persuaded by inflated peer evaluations and therefore may not honestly and accurately evaluate themselves.[23] Regarding the method for self-evaluation, Bergee and Cecconi-Roberts found that having students listen to themselves on high-quality, digital audio recordings was just as effective as using videotapes.

## 2002—Junior High Band Students Demonstrated a Need for Teacher Input Regarding Accuracy in Self-Evaluations of Music Performance.

Michael Hewitt created a student self-evaluation form by adapting the woodwind and brass solo evaluation form (WBSEF) developed by Saunders and Holahan.[24] In Hewitt's study, junior high instrumentalists used the form independently, with little input from teachers. Model recordings were provided for students to use as standards for self-evaluation. Apparently, the self-guided form for self-evaluation was not sufficient for students to develop self-evaluation accuracy, even when a model recording was used as a standard. Hewitt found that students evaluated their playing more highly than did their teachers and that students' ability to accurately self-evaluate did not improve over time when teacher involvement was not present. Hewitt suggested that "it may be necessary for junior high band directors to instruct students systematically in self-evaluation on an ongoing basis."[25] Because students' self-evaluation accuracy did not increase over the limited, five-session time frame of the study, Hewitt proposed that extended and frequent opportunities to self-evaluate over time might be necessary to help students develop self-evaluation accuracy.[26]

## 2003—In An Investigative Study, the Ability to Accurately Self-Evaluate Served as a Predictor of Growth in Improvisational Abilities Among Jazz Players.

In a study of instrumental jazz improvisation among players in university jazz ensembles, Lissa May found a greater level of self-evaluation accuracy than did Bergee and Hewitt in previous studies. For May, self-evaluation emerged as the most dependable predictor of achievement in instrumental jazz improvisation. Instrumentalists in May's study self-evaluated on a simple three-point scale regarding jazz-improvisation ability as follows: (1) beginner, (2) moderate ability, or (3) advanced.

Based on results, May found a significant relationship between self-evaluation accuracy and jazz-improvisation achievement.[27]

## 2004—Researchers Successfully Used Recorded Models to Help Students Achieve Self-Evaluation Accuracy.

It is generally known that the practice of listening to model recordings aids music learners in self-evaluation. Morrison, Montemayor, and Wiltshire found that students who self-evaluated against a standard presented in a model recording were able to develop awareness of deficiencies in their individual and ensemble playing. Middle school, junior high, and high school instrumentalists in the study offered a greater number of comments in self-evaluations of their playing when a recorded model was available. According to the researchers, "the presence of a model . . . may have allowed students to maintain a more consistent or objective perspective according to which they measured their progress."[28]

## 2011—In An Experimental Study of Self-Evaluation Among Middle School Instrumentalists, Accuracy in Self-Evaluation Remained Elusive.

Michael Hewitt found that when middle school band students received instruction in how to self-evaluate, it had little impact on both self-evaluation accuracy and music performance. He noted that this result is not in agreement with findings of researchers in math and narrative-writing education.[29] It is not known, yet, why self-evaluation accuracy appears to elude music students, as evidenced in numerous studies. In Hewitt's 2011 study, it is interesting to note that students who received self-evaluation instruction were able to perform as well as students who spent all of their class time in rehearsing. In other words, the class time spent on self-evaluation instruction did not take away from students' acquisition of performance skills.[30] One might speculate that frequent instruction and opportunities for self-evaluation over an extended period of time might result in improved self-evaluation accuracy for students in music-performance classes.[31]

## PRACTICAL APPLICATIONS AND INSTRUCTIONAL STRATEGIES FOR SELF-EVALUATION IN MUSIC LEARNING

Researchers note that meaningful self-evaluation does not occur when students are left to their own devices to pass judgment on their work. Students need to be taught how to self-evaluate, and they need guidance from teachers. Even then, it is difficult for inexperienced music students to accurately self-evaluate. Some researchers suggest that accuracy in self-evaluation might result from extended exposure to exemplary performance models along with expert guidance from music teachers who can guide their students to focus on particular aspects of music learning and performance, thereby providing structure for self-evaluation activities. According to Farrell, self-evaluation helps music learners to "investigate their strengths and weaknesses, become aware of their personal growth and creative potential, and develop a realization and respect for the artistic process while considering their relationship to it."[32]

### Music-Learning Scenarios for Student Self-Evaluation

Let us imagine a scenario in which second-grade general-music students are asked to evaluate their efforts and achievements in response to their teacher's questions at the end of class. The music teacher asks, "Did you put forth your best effort in music class today? How? Did you learn something new in music today? What? Did you improve your music ability today? In what way? Will you be a better musician because of what you learned today? How?" Students respond by raising their

---

**Tips for Teachers**

Ask students to create their own rubrics for self-evaluation. This job can be done in cooperative learning groups. As students work together to create rubrics, they will be required to identify important performance goals and to consider desired levels of achievement. In small-group collaborations, students can share their thoughts about what constitutes successful achievement of musical goals.

hands, giving thumbs-up or thumbs-down signals, and participating in
a brief classroom discussion. The self-evaluation takes only a few minutes and provides closure at the end of music class. It allows students
to complete the metacognitive-learning cycle (planning, monitoring,
evaluating), thereby laying the foundation for continued learning in the
next class session.

In another scenario, we might consider students in a middle school
choir who are preparing for adjudicated performance at a music festival. The director makes copies of the adjudication form and distributes
them to his students. He explains the rating scale and criteria listed on
the form, providing definitions for terms such as *diction, intonation,
vocal tone,* and *stage presence.* He leads students in a discussion of
what makes an excellent choral performance and reinforces important
criteria on which judges will rate the ensemble. When the director feels
confident that students understand how they will be judged, he makes a
good-quality recording of a rehearsal run-through of festival repertoire.
He plays back the recording while students fill out the adjudication
form to evaluate their own choir. Following this activity, the director
invites students to share their ratings on specific criteria with the class.
Most importantly, he asks students to substantiate their ratings and
comments, requiring them to engage in analysis of their performance.
Together, the students brainstorm a list of strengths and weaknesses
of the choir. The director writes the list on a large chart that will hang
on the wall of the choir room. He asks students to offer ideas about
strategies for overcoming weaknesses in the days leading up to festival
performance. Next to each weakness on the chart, the director writes
at least one strategy offered by students for correcting the problem.
Additionally, he requires students to acknowledge their strengths and
offer suggestions about how the ensemble can make the most of its
positive qualities. He writes these suggestions on the chart, too. The
director leaves the chart hanging on the classroom wall throughout the
time leading up to festival. He refers to it frequently during rehearsals,
reminding students that the list of strengths and weaknesses and suggestions for improvement was created from student input. In this way,
students feel involved in the process of preparing for adjudicated performance. The metacognitive skills of self-awareness, self-evaluation,
goal setting, and strategy planning are evidenced in this scenario.

In a final scenario, let us imagine a group of students in a piano class who are working at their own pace through exercises and pieces of repertoire in beginning or intermediate method books. Some of the students are new to piano study, while others have completed previous semesters of piano classes or lessons. Due to the individual nature of their work, the teacher will grade each student on effort and relative progress made throughout a marking period. Although the teacher will take responsibility for assigning final grades, it is beneficial for students to reflect on their own effort and progress. For this reason, the teacher prepares self-evaluation rubrics for students to use in setting goals and evaluating their own progress throughout a semester of piano study.

## Sample Rubrics, Rating Scales, and Checklists for Student Self-Evaluation in Music Classes

Figure 5.1 shows a self-evaluation rubric for students in a high school or college music theory class.[33] A Likert-scale format is used. The rubric is holistic and qualitative. Rather than rating specific music theory skills, students are asked to make an overall assessment of their efforts and strategies in the class. Students might make a self-evaluation such as this at several points throughout a semester. Following self-evaluation activities, the teacher might encourage students to follow up by devising strategies for improvement and seeking extra help when needed.

Figure 5.2 shows an adaptation of the National Music Adjudication Coalition Concert Band or Orchestra Music Assessment Form.[34] I have modified it for student self-evaluation regarding ensemble performance. A numerical rating scale is used. In addition to rating their current performance abilities, students are asked to devise strategies for future improvement. Students can fill out the self-evaluation form as they listen to an audio recording or watch a video of their band or orchestra in rehearsal or performance. For maximum effect, the band/orchestra director might want to spend some time defining the criteria and explaining musical elements that students should listen for.

Figure 5.3 shows a quantitative, analytic rubric for self-evaluation of sightsinging achievement. It is analytic rather than holistic because criteria are delineated in discrete categories, such as pitch and rhythm. It is quantitative rather than qualitative because a numerical-rating scale

Music Theory Self-Evaluation

Name: _____. Date: _____

Circle your response to each item.

**1. I rate my current progress in music theory as:**

Excellent          Satisfactory          Needs improvement

**2. I rate my homework record in music theory as:**

Excellent          Satisfactory          Needs improvement

**3. I rate my test/quiz record in music theory as:**

Excellent          Satisfactory          Needs improvement

**4. I accomplish music theory learning tasks on time and in a manner that facilitates steady progress in the class.**

Strongly agree          Agree          Neutral          Disagree          Strongly disagree

**5. I am able to accurately perceive my personal strengths and weaknesses related to music theory.**

Strongly agree          Agree          Neutral          Disagree          Strongly disagree

**6. I am able to devise successful cognitive strategies to accomplish learning tasks in music theory.**

Strongly agree          Agree          Neutral          Disagree          Strongly disagree

**7. I seek and receive help from my teacher or a tutor when needed.**

Strongly agree          Agree          Neutral          Disagree          Strongly disagree

**8. I share cognitive strategies with my learning partner in study sessions at least once per week.**

Strongly agree          Agree          Neutral          Disagree          Strongly disagree

**Figure 5.1. Music-Theory Self-Evaluation**

is used. Students are asked to assess strengths and weaknesses and to suggest strategies for improvement.

Figure 5.4 shows a rubric for student self-evaluation of a choral-performing ensemble. I have adapted it from an adjudication form used by a state chapter of the National Association for Music Education.[35] It is analytic and qualitative. Students are asked to write narrative comments regarding eight criteria for choral performance. Rather than giving numerical scores, students are asked to reinforce comments by assigning

**Student Evaluation of Band/Orchestra Performance**

Student's Name: _____ Date: _____

Band/Orchestra Class: _____ Class Period: _____

Directions: Fill in the rubric below, giving points for the stated criteria. Add up the points for individual categories, and indicate total points. Devise a personal strategy for improvement.

| Category | Description | Possible Points | Points Given Today |
|---|---|---|---|
| Tone Quality | Natural, Free from tension, Blend, Energetic, Controlled | 0-15 | |
| Pitch | Accuracy Intonation | 0-15 | |
| Technique | Attacks, Accents, Missed notes, Releases, Articulation/Bowing | 0-15 | |
| Rhythm | Accuracy, Tempo, Steady pulse | 0-15 | |
| Interpretation and Musicianship | Correct style, Balance, Artistry, Sense of ensemble, Expressivity, Nuance, Communicating with a Sense of Purpose | 0-15 | |
| Dynamics | Use of full range (*pp-ff*), Use of subtle dynamic changes | 0-10 | |
| Breath/Mallet/Bow Management | Phrasing, Supports tone, Carefully Planned and Executed | 0-10 | |
| Stage Deportment | Attitude, Appearance, Confidence, Posture | 0-5 | |
| | | | TOTAL POINTS: |

In the space below, briefly describe at least one thing that you will personally do in the next week to raise the performance quality of our band/orchestra.

**Figure 5.2.   Self-Evaluation Band/Orchestra**

a letter grade for each criterion. Using the form, students might self-evaluate the ensemble after watching a video recording of the ensemble in performance. In fact, students could watch and listen more than once to allow time to make thoughtful and appropriate comments. To make the self-evaluation a productive activity, the choral director might need to define terms and explain criteria. Following the self-evaluation activity,

**Sight-Singing Self-Evaluation via Voice Recording**

Name _____ Date _____

Sight-singing Exercise # ____, page ____.

Directions – Listen to your audio recording of the assigned sight-singing exercise. Read each criterion in the rubric. Give yourself a rating on a scale from 0 to 3 points. A rating of 'zero' means that you did not sing at all. Points from 1 through 3 indicate levels of achievement: 1 = Needs improvement; 2 = Good; 3 = Excellent. Circle a score for each criterion. Tally all points for your final score.

1. Pitch accuracy                                          0  1  2  3

2. Rhythm accuracy                                      0  1  2  3

3. Accurate use of solfeggio                          0  1  2  3

4. Reading notes quickly and accurately          0  1  2  3

5. Maintaining steady beat and tempo             0  1  2  3

Total score = ____

What is your greatest current strength in sight-singing?

What is your greatest current weakness in sight-singing?

Explain at least one strategy for personal improvement in sight-singing.

**Figure 5.3.   Sight-Singing Self-Evaluation**

the choral director might lead a class discussion in which students share their comments and suggestions for improvement.

Figure 5.5 shows a simple, holistic, and qualitative rubric for student self-evaluation that might be used for younger music learners in general-music classes or beginning-level performance ensembles. The lack of music terminology and specific criteria leaves the self-evaluation open to interpretation by students and their music teacher. When using a rubric such as this, the teacher might want to lead a class discussion regarding specific criteria and focus points for self-evaluation.

**Student Self-Evaluation of Choral Ensemble Performance**

Name _____. Date _____.

Directions – watch the video of your choir in rehearsal or performance. Consider the criteria listed below. Write at least one comment for each criterion. Be sure to consider positive as well as negative qualities of the choir's performance. In the box next to each criterion, give a letter grade: A, B, C, D, or E.

TONE (beauty, control) _____

_____

INTONATION _____ ☐

_____

DICTION (clarity of consonants, purity of vowels) _____ ☐

_____

TECHNIQUE (accuracy of notes, breathing, posture, rhythm) _____ ☐

_____

BALANCE (between sections, within section) _____ ☐

_____

INTERPRETATION (expression, phrasing, style) _____ ☐

_____

OVERAL EFFECT (appearance, vitality, stage presence) _____ ☐

_____

In the space below, describe at least one strategy for improving your choir's performance.

**Figure 5.4.   Self-Evaluation, Choral Singing**

---

**Music-Making Self-Evaluation**

Name _____ Date _____

How would you rate your music-making today?

Give yourself one BRAVO! ☺ What did you do well in music today? Write about it.

_____

_____

_____

Think of how you can improve your music-making in the future. Write 3 suggestions.

1. _____

2. _____

3. _____

Good 👍 Job!

---

**Figure 5.5.  Self-Evaluation, General Music**

The purpose of the "Bravo" is to encourage students to focus on positive aspects of their music making. The section regarding suggestions for improvement is included to encourage students to engage in the metacognitive skill of planning strategies for future learning.

Student self-evaluation can be a formal or informal activity, based on the needs of music learners, the learning goals for particular music classes, and the time and resources available to music teachers. Whether it involves a brief class discussion or a more formal activity, such as filling out a rating sheet, student self-evaluation might become a regular part of music classes. As evidenced in numerous research studies, music students frequently evaluate themselves differently from the way their teachers evaluate them. Sometimes students appear to have inflated views of their musical accomplishments. It appears that the ability to hold an exemplary model in mind and to accurately rate one's approximations toward excellence is a skill that many students lack. This ability sometimes eludes music students from beginning through college levels. Nevertheless, researchers and music educators appear to agree that student self-evaluation is a worthwhile activity and that the pursuit of self-evaluation accuracy is a worthwhile goal. Especially in light of a desire to impart lifelong music-making skills to students, music teachers will continue to assist learners in developing the metacognitive skill of self-evaluation.

## NOTES

1. Judy Cunningham, Carol Krull, Nora Land, and Sylvia Russell, "Motivating Students to be Self-Reflective Learners through Goal-Setting and Self-Evaluation" (Action Research Project, Saint Xavier University and Skylight Professional Development, 2000), 7.

2. Ibid., 20–25.

3. Randall E. Aitchison, "The Effects of Self-Evaluation Techniques on the Musical Performance, Self-Evaluation Accuracy, Motivation, and Self-Esteem of Middle School Instrumental Music Students" (Ph.D. diss., University of Iowa, ProQuest UMI Dissertations Publishing, 1995, 304196547), 7; Robert J. Marzano, *A Different Kind of Classroom: Teaching with Dimensions of Learning* (Alexandria, Va.: Association for Supervision and Curriculum Development, 1992), 131.

4. Connie L. Hale, and Susan K. Green, "Six Key Principles for Music Assessment," *Music Educators Journal* 95, no. 4 (2009): 29.

5. Chris Masui and Erik DeCorte, "Enhancing Learning and Problem Solving Skills: Orienting and Self-Judging, Two Powerful and Trainable Learning Tools," *Learning and Instruction* 9 (1999): 521.

6. Lyle Davidson and Larry Scripp, "Tracing Reflective Thinking in the Performance Ensemble," *Quarterly Journal of Music Teaching and Learning* 1, no. 1 (1990): 60.

7. Ibid., 53.

8. Ibid., 60.

9. Martin J. Bergee, "A Comparison of Faculty, Peer, and Self-Evaluation of Applied Brass Jury Performances," *Journal of Research in Music Education* 41, no. 1 (1993): 20.

10. Ibid., 26.

11. Aitchison, "The Effects of Self-Evaluation," 122–23.

12. Ibid., 197.

13. Ibid., 215–16.

14. Marilyn J. Kostka, "Effects of Self-Assessment and Successive Approximations on 'Knowing' and 'Valuing' Selected Keyboard Skills," *Journal of Research in Music Education* 45, no. 2 (1997): 275.

15. Ibid., 277–79.

16. Ibid., 280.

17. Michael P. Hewitt, "The Effects of Modeling, Self-Evaluation, and Self-Listening on Junior High Instrumentalists' Music Performance and Practice Attitude," *Journal of Research in Music Education* 49, no. 4 (2001): 318–19.

18. Ryan Daniel, "Self-Assessment in Performance," *British Journal of Music Education* 18, no. 3 (2001): 219.

19. Ibid., 223–24.

20. Ibid., 225.

21. Martin J. Bergee and Lecia Cecconi-Roberts, "Effects of Small-Group Peer Interaction on Self-Evaluation of Music Performance," *Journal of Research in Music Education* 50, no. 3 (2002): 266.

22. Ibid., 265.

23. Ibid., 266.

24. Michael P. Hewitt, "Self-Evaluation Tendencies of Junior High Instrumentalists," *Journal of Research in Music Education* 50, no. 3 (2002): 218.

25. Ibid., 222.

26. Ibid., 223–24.

27. Lissa F. May, "Factors and Abilities Influencing Achievement in Instrumental Jazz Improvisation," *Journal of Research in Music Education* 51, no. 3 (2003): 254.

28. Steven J. Morrison, Mark Montemayor, and Eric S. Wiltshire, "The Effect of a Recorded Model on Band Students' Performance Self-Evaluations, Achievement and Attitude," *Journal of Research in Music Education* 52, no. 2 (2004): 126.

29. Michael P. Hewitt, "The Impact of Self-Evaluation Instruction on Student Self-Evaluation, Music Performance, and Self-Evaluation Accuracy," *Journal of Research in Music Education* 59, no. 1 (2011): 13–16.

30. Ibid., 16.

31. Ibid.

32. Susan Farrell, *Tools for Powerful Student Evaluation* (Ft. Lauderdale, Fla.: Meredith Music Publications, 1997), 21.

33. Carol Benton, "A Study of the Effects of Metacognition on Student Learning Outcomes among Students in College Music Theory Classes" (paper presented at the College Music Society Southern Chapter Regional Conference, Tampa, Fla., February 24, 2012).

34. MENC, "National Music Adjudication Coalition Concert Band or Orchestra Music Assessment Form," http://musiced.nafme.org/files/2013/02/NMAC bandorchestraform.pdf (accessed December 17, 2013) (accessed September 4, 2011).

35. Georgia Music Educators Association, "Choral Large Group Adjudication Form," http://opus.gmea.org/Pages/Forum/ViewForum.aspx?Forum=5 (accessed July 8, 2012).

# 6

# SOCIALLY SHARED METACOGNITION: THINKING ALOUD IN MUSIC LEARNING

In general, metacognition is an internal, covert, mental activity. Therefore, it is necessary for teachers to bring metacognition out into the open through instructional strategies such as having students write critiques, self-evaluations, or reflections on learning. With structure and guidance, learners engage in metacognition and teachers are able to glimpse their students' inner thought processes by reading reflections and self-evaluations. It is not always necessary, however, to engage in writing activities to make metacognition active and evident. Metacognition becomes overt and visible when learners participate in focused classroom discussions or work on learning tasks together in pairs or small groups.

With teacher guidance, learners can explain their thought processes, problem-solving procedures, and learning strategies to each other, thereby reaping the benefits of socially shared metacognition. We know that metacognition involves monitoring and control of one's own thought processes, actions, and products of effort in learning tasks. Social metacognition involves learning partners or members of small groups who monitor and control each other's problem-solving processes, actions, and products of effort in shared learning tasks. When learners share verbal descriptions of their thought processes with their peers, improved individual thinking appears as a beneficial by-product.[1]

A common term for socially shared metacognition is *thinking aloud*. When students are asked to think aloud, they begin to engage in "deliberate introspection," an activity that leads to greater awareness of themselves as learners.[2] Numerous educational researchers advocate the practice of having learners verbalize their thought processes while they are engaged in learning tasks.[3] Because metacognition is manifested in thinking aloud, think-aloud protocol is used by investigative researchers exploring how persons think when solving a problem or completing a learning task.[4] Likewise, it allows teachers to follow the thought processes of their students.

When learners think aloud with partners while completing learning tasks, the following changes are likely to occur:[5]

- Learners become more aware of their own thought processes and more in control of those processes.
- Learners become more thorough and give more attention to accuracy.
- Learners become more active participants in learning, rather than learning by rote and waiting to have information fed to them by their teachers.
- As learners become more self-aware and receive feedback from their learning partners, they can diagnose problems and make corrections.
- Working together, learning partners discover challenges and difficulties and devise strategies for overcoming them.

---

### Tips for Teachers

Although classroom management is a top priority, allowing students to talk among themselves for specific discussions and for controlled periods of time can be beneficial. If students are required to explain their musical thought processes to their peers, then brief periods of talking to other students can result in enriched learning experiences through socially shared metacognition. By carefully planning and monitoring the discussion sessions among students, teachers can maintain control of the learning environment.

Thinking aloud to apply metacognition in learning situations is not merely a matter of randomly verbalizing a stream of consciousness; therefore, it is important for teachers to provide structure for think-aloud sessions when students work with learning partners or in small groups. Without structure imposed by the teacher, students' conversations are likely to veer off task, and metacognitive skills will not be employed. Teachers might carefully instruct their students to explain their thought processes, procedures, and actions to their peers as they work through learning tasks. This type of self-explanation requires a high degree of self-reflection in an ongoing manner. Teachers can promote self-explanation by asking thought-provoking questions, such as "How did you know that?" "Can you tell me how you got that answer?" or "Why are you doing that?" As a benefit, the habit of self-explanation appears to remain with learners, even when they are not being directly questioned by a teacher or a learning partner.[6]

When students engage in social metacognition, they distribute metacognitive responsibilities among members of a group. Group members can observe each other at work and provide peer evaluations.[7] Distribution of metacognitive responsibility allows learners who are strong in certain areas of a discipline to help their peers who might be weak in those areas. This reciprocal effect results in improved cognition for each individual through focusing of attention and capitalizing on individual strengths.[8]

An additional advantage of social metacognition is improved motivation. Because distribution of responsibilities occurs when students practice social metacognition, the risks to the individual are lessened. The individual learner receives emotional support from peers during the learning process, resulting in greater motivation for the learning task. This phenomenon is known as *reciprocal scaffolding.*[9] *Self-scaffolding* occurs among learners when they engage in the metacognitive processes of planning, organizing, and goal setting for learning experiences. In pairs or groups, students engage in reciprocal scaffolding as they share these responsibilities to build knowledge together and to recognize accurate or inaccurate knowledge and skills among their peers. Reciprocal scaffolding results in greater levels of motivation.[10]

**Photo 6.1.   Fourth Grade–Composer Posters**

## OVERVIEW OF RESEARCH ON SOCIALLY SHARED METACOGNITION

### 2008—In a Study Conducted Among Middle School Band Students, Discourse (Talking) During Rehearsals Emerged as an Influential Factor in Student Achievement.

Teryl Dobbs explored the role of discourse (talking) during band rehearsals. He recorded and analyzed verbal communications between and among his students and himself. Dobbs based his study on the following premises regarding connections between language and cognition:

1. Language is linked to cognition.
2. Higher-order thinking is language dependent.
3. One's comprehension of the world depends on one's habitual language use.
4. Language and thought are irrevocably entwined with culture and context.
5. The language that one utilizes provides structure for cognition.[11]

Dobbs concluded that "students in every type of music classroom need the discursive space where their voices can be heard, a space with ample opportunities to articulate and mediate their musical understandings. Students require discursive openings to make their own musical decisions and to act as musical experts so that they may take an active role in their learning processes.[12]"

## 2009—In Elementary School Classrooms, Socially Shared Metacognition was Used to Help Young English-Language Learners Become Active and Accountable Participants in Learning.

Daric Desautel investigated metacognition among students in prekindergarten through second grade. In addition to being in their first years of school, 80 percent of the children were learning English as a second language. Desautel found that "although metacognitive knowledge may not depend on oral language ability, a robust vocabulary greatly helps young students develop and articulate it."[13] Interestingly, students who had difficulty with verbal expressions of their own thought processes were able to successfully verbalize the same procedures when they were explaining learning tasks to their peers. Based on results of the study, Desautel described metacognition as both interpersonal and intrapersonal and concluded that shared metacognition in communal goal setting enables students to develop a sense of accountability for learning.[14]

## 2009—In the Academic Area of Teaching Reading, Researchers Used the Strategy of Self-Explanation to Help Readers Develop Better Comprehension.

Through an extensive review of literature, McNamara and Magliano found that learners who engaged in self-explanation tended to understand more from their reading than did learners who did not self-explain. Self-explanation is prompted by a teacher and stimulates metacognitive reflection in the learner or reader. It is closely related to thinking aloud but differs in that students are specifically required to explain what they comprehend from their reading tasks.[15] Based on the premise that students who exhibit better metacognitive skills tend to be more successful in reading comprehension, McNamara and Magliano required learners in two studies to engage in self-explanation. This task, in turn, required learners to assess their own levels of comprehension and then to consider the difficulty level of the reading assignments and relative success of their selected reading or studying strategies. Upon self-assessment, learners might choose to employ different reading strategies. Furthermore, learners were required to verbally explain these processes.[16] The researchers concluded that verbal self-explanation (thinking aloud) served as one of several helpful metacognitive strategies that aided readers in developing better comprehension.[17]

## 2012—In an Exploratory Study Among College Music-Theory Students, Think-Aloud Sessions with Partners Were Employed as a Strategy for Learning.

In a study of metacognition among college music-theory students, Benton found that participants perceived benefits from think-aloud sessions with learning partners. Participants reported that when they were required to explain their thinking processes, they gained clarity and insight for solving music-theory problems.[18]

## THINKING ALOUD IN MUSIC CLASSES

The instructional strategy of having learners think aloud with partners, in small groups, or in classroom discussions is one that fits some (but not all) music-learning situations. Obviously, band, choir, or orchestra directors do not want their singers and players talking to each other in the middle of rehearsals. Although some amount of controlled discussion for collaborative problem solving among singers or players is appropriate and beneficial in rehearsals, it would not be advantageous to launch into an extended think-aloud session while trying to develop artistry for performance of repertoire. In that situation, less talk and more music making is the ideal. Music learning is not a cognitive, linguistic, or mathematic type of learning, and in many situations music learning must be approached as a nonverbal, aural experience.[19]

Reimer emphasized the distinction between the widely accepted concept of "knowing" and "meaning" as language-related and language dependent and the musical concept of "knowing" and "meaning" as perceived through experiencing musical sound.[20] In fact, language can interfere with the pure experience of music. "Musical creation explores and forms the feelingful qualities of sounds. This exploring-forming process is not a process of encoding messages."[21] Surely, there is a place for *not* talking in music learning, and think-aloud instructional strategies might be detrimental to music learning in many situations.

There are many music-learning experiences, however, in which it might be productive for students to engage in socially shared metacognition in the form of think-aloud sessions. The following is a list of some situations where music teachers might want to implement think-aloud sessions among learning partners or in small groups.

- *Music-theory class.* Learning tasks in music theory often take the form of pencil-and-paper, problem-solving activities. Think-aloud sessions are beneficial for students working on music-theory assignments. Learners can explain their thought processes as they work through theory exercises, and their peers can provide feedback.
- *Reading and writing music notation.* For younger students who are not yet ready for music theory, simple exercises in learning to read and write music notation can be completed in think-aloud sessions. These might take the form of pencil-paper activities, or the activities might involve working with manipulative objects. Learners can think aloud, describing their thought processes with partners or small groups as they learn to read and write music notation.
- *Score study for sight-reading exercises.* It is advantageous for music learners to quickly peruse a score (noting elements such as key and meter signatures, melodic and harmonic characteristics, and potential "tricky" spots) before singing or playing an exercise or piece of repertoire. This preliminary perusal can be enriched when students work with learning partners in brief think-aloud sessions. As music learners explain their thought processes to their learning partners, they are able to clarify their thoughts before attempting to perform a sight-reading exercise.
- *Composition activities in general-music classes.* Students might work in pairs or small groups to critique their peers' compositions and help each other achieve music composition goals. Teachers

---

**Tips for Teachers**

Music teachers may want to assign *think-aloud* learning partners within their classes. More-advanced players or singers might be paired with those who are on a beginning level and need extra help. Conversely, teachers might want to pair advanced students together to work independently on more challenging assignments while teachers work with students who need assistance. Either way, the think-aloud format can be useful for certain types of music learning.

---

might provide scripted questions for young composers to ask each other as they explore their creativity. Learning partners might be taught to question each other regarding specific choices and decisions to be made during the composition process.

- *Basic playing techniques for beginning instrumentalists.* In the beginning stages of learning to play an instrument, students must overcome difficulties in several areas, such as assembling their instruments, positioning and posture, developing a correct embouchure, and learning basic fingering. It might be helpful for students to work in pairs or small groups in think-aloud sessions regarding these challenges. Teachers might provide a list of questions that students could ask each other as they work through basic routines and establish productive habits for instrumental playing. By explaining their thought processes to each other, beginning students might clarify important basic procedures.

## IMPLEMENTING A THINK-ALOUD SESSION

In this section, we will explore a how-to guide to implementing a think-aloud activity with students in a music class. Procedures are based on the Thinkback program developed by Jack Lochhead.[22] The key element is "Thinking Aloud Pair Problem Solving (TAPPS)."[23] The term *thinkback* refers to the way in which thinking aloud during problem solving allows learners to become aware of their thought processes. This phenomenon is similar to the way in which a video-recorded *playback* allows athletes to become aware of their physical movements during sports plays.[24] In a think-aloud session based on TAPPS, students work in pairs. One partner is designated as the active learner, engaged in a problem-solving learning task. The other partner is instructed to ask thought-provoking questions of the learner and to keep the learner talking throughout the problem-solving process. After a problem has been solved, students switch roles before moving on to the next problem. The previous learner becomes the listener, and vice versa.[25]

Figure 6.1 provides a script of questions that might be asked by the listener partner during a think-aloud session for sight-singing.[26] In a choral-music classroom, the teacher would provide a script such as this for students acting in the role of listeners. By asking the scripted questions, listeners guide learners through an established set of steps for

---

Scripted Questions for the "Listener" during a Sight-Singing Think-Aloud Session

1. What is the key of the exercise? How do you know?

2. What is the tonal center, or "do"? How do you know?

3. What is the starting pitch? Is it "do", or another note in the scale?

4. Does your part move mostly by step or by skip? Does it move mostly upward or downward? Do you see any tricky places in the melodic contour of your part? Do you see any difficult intervals in your part? Do you see any places where your part creates a dissonant interval with another part?

5. Do you see any measures that are exactly alike? Do you see any measures that are similar, but not the same?

6. Can you say the solfege names of the notes in your part? Say them for me.

7. What is the meter? How many beats are in each measure? How do you know? What kind of note will get one beat? How do you know?

8. What is the shortest note value that you see in the exercise?

9. What is the longest note value that you see in the exercise?

10. Can you tap the rhythm of your part as you speak the solfege names in rhythm? Do that for me.

---

**Figure 6.1. Think-Aloud Listener's Script**

preparing to perform a sight-singing exercise. The procedure should take only about three minutes. After performing one exercise, students would switch roles with their partners to prepare and perform a different exercise.

## Teacher's Script for a Sight-singing Think Aloud in a Choral-Music Class

The following script for a choral-music teacher illustrates procedures for leading a think-aloud session during a typical sight-singing portion of a high school choral-music rehearsal.[27] Because class time is precious and directors often feel pressured to spend the majority of allotted time on repertoire rehearsal, the parameters of the think-aloud sight-singing session are specifically designed to take only about ten to twelve minutes. Additionally, it should be noted that the following example includes the use of two Bach chorales that can be downloaded free of charge from the Choral Public Domain Library;[28] however, any sight-singing exercises might be used.

> TEACHER: 1. First, find a partner. Move around if you need to sit next to someone who will be your learning partner for the sight-singing task.
> 2. Now you are sitting next to your learning partner. The person on the right of your pair will be Partner 1, and the person on the left of your pair will be Partner 2.
> 3. Partner 1 will be the learner. Partner 2 will be the listener. Raise your hand if you are the learner. Raise your hand if you are the listener. [*The teacher checks to see if students are ready to begin.*]
> 4. I will distribute a sight-singing exercise, face down. Every learner needs to take one of the papers. I will also distribute a script of questions for listeners. Every listener needs to look at the script to see the questions that you should ask of the learner.
> 5. When I give the signal, all of the learners will turn their sight-singing papers over and begin to study the exercise. I will play the scale and cadence to establish tonality. You will have three minutes to figure out how to sing your part. You may use solfeggio or numbers. During your three-minute preparation time, the listener will ask the learner several thought-provoking questions, according to the script. The learner will respond to the questions and *think aloud* while preparing to sing the exercise. At the end of three minutes, I will again play the scale and

cadence and give a signal to begin singing. All of the learners will sight-sing their parts.

6. Following the first singing, learners will have a one-minute period to reflect and self-assess, talking to their partners. They will tell their partners about any mistakes they made and will strategize ways to improve their performance.
7. After the one-minute self-assessment think-aloud, the learners will sing the exercise one more time and will tell their partners if they think they made improvements.
8. We will repeat the entire think-aloud process with a different sight-singing exercise in which the partners will change roles. Partner 1 will become the listener, and Partner 2 will become the learner.
9. Ready? Let's begin.

## Teacher's Instructional Procedures

1. Distribute the Bach chorale, *Ach Gott und Herr, wie Gross und Schwer*.[29] Be sure that each learner gets a copy. Be sure that papers are face down. Distribute scripts of questions to listeners.
2. Give the signal to begin the three-minute think-aloud preparation time. Play a C major scale and cadence to establish tonality.
3. Call time after three minutes. Play a scale and cadence. Count off, and conduct the singing.
4. Allow time for a one-minute think-aloud self-assessment.
5. Play a cadence. Count off, and conduct singers in their second try.
6. Switch roles. The original listener becomes the learner. The original learner becomes the new listener. Begin the process anew:

1. Distribute the Bach chorale, *Alle Menschen Müssen Sterben*.[30]
2. Follow the above steps as before. Establish a D major tonality.
3. Continue steps 3 through 6 as described above.

Although the example described here is specific to a secondary-level choral-music class, the procedures for think-aloud sessions might be adapted and used in other types of music classes. Instrumental-ensemble directors, music-theory teachers, general-music teachers, or applied-music teachers might find that their students benefit from occasionally participating in think-aloud sessions. Although a think-aloud session might not be appropriate during a rehearsal of repertoire, the process is particularly beneficial when students are required to engage in problem-solving tasks related to music learning.

## NOTES

1. Ming Ming Chiu and Sze Wing Kuo, "Social Metacognition in Groups: Benefits, Difficulties, Learning, and Teaching," in *Metacognition: New Research Developments*, edited by Clayton B. Larson (New York: Nova Science Publishers, 2009), 117.

2. D. N. Perkins, *The Mind's Best Work* (Cambridge, Mass.: Harvard University Press, 1981), 38.

3. John Dunlosky and Janet Metcalfe, *Metacognition* (Thousand Oaks, Calif.: SAGE Publications, 2009), 222–24; Jack Lochhead, "Sound Thinking with Thinkback 2000" (paper presented at the Technological Education and National Development Conference, "Crossroads of the Millennium," April 8–10, 2000, Abu Dhabi, United Arab Emirates), 5–6; Hope J. Hartman, "Developing Students' Metacognitive Knowledge and Skills," in *Metacognition in Learning and Instruction: Theory, Research and Practice*, edited by Hope J. Hartman (Dordrecht, Netherlands: Kluwer Academic Publishers, 2001), 59–63; Gregory Schraw, Kent J. Crippen, and Kendall Hartley, "Promoting Self-Regulation in Science Education: Metacognition as Part of a Broader Perspective on Learning," *Research in Science Education* 36 (2006): 120; Arthur Whimbey, "Students Can Learn to Be Better Problem Solvers," *Educational Leadership* 37, no. 7 (1980): 560–62.

4. Perkins, *Mind's Best Work*, 32–35.

5. Hartman, "Developing Students' Metacognitive Knowledge," 60–61.

6. Dunlosky and Metcalfe, *Metacognition*, 224.

7. Chiu and Kuo, "Social Metacognition," 120.

8. Ibid.

9. Ibid., 119.

10. Ibid.

11. Teryl L. Dobbs, "Discourse in the Band Room: The Role of Talk in an Instrumental Music Classroom," in *Diverse Methodologies in the Study of Music Teaching and Learning*, edited by Linda K. Thompson and Mark Robin Campbell (Charlotte, N.C.: Information Age Publishing, 2008), 140.

12. Ibid., 155.

13. Daric Desautel, "Becoming a Thinking Thinker: Metacognition, Self-Reflection, and Classroom Practice," *Teachers College Record* 111, no. 8 (2009): 2015.

14. Ibid.

15. Danielle S. McNamara and Joseph P. Magliano, "The Dynamics of Reading," in *Handbook of Metacognition in Education*, edited by Douglas J. Hacker, John Dunlosky, and Arthur C. Graesser (New York: Routledge, 2009), 61–62.

16. Ibid., 73–74.

17. Ibid., 77.

18. Carol Benton, "A Study of the Effects of Metacognition on Student Learning Outcomes among Students in College Music Theory Classes" (paper presented at the College Music Society Southern Chapter Regional Conference, Tampa, Fla., February 24, 2012).

19. Daniel Kohut, *Musical Performance: Learning Theory and Pedagogy* (Englewood Cliffs, N.J.: Prentice-Hall, 1985), 8–9.

20. Bennett Reimer, *A Philosophy of Music Education: Advancing the Vision* (Upper Saddle River, N.J.: Pearson Education, 2003), 135.

21. Ibid., 137.

22. Lochhead, "Sound Thinking," 4.

23. Ibid.

24. Ibid., 5.

25. Ibid., 6–9.

26. Carol Benton, "But, What Will They Think? Strategies for Promoting Metacognition among Students in Music Classes and Performing Ensembles" (interest session, Georgia Music Educators Association In-Service Conference, Savannah, Ga., January 2011).

27. Ibid.

28. Choral Public Domain Library, http://www3.cpdl.org/wiki/index.php/Main_Page.

29. Johann Sebastian Bach, *Ach Gott und Herr, wie Gross und Schwer*, BWV 255, edited by Claudio Macchi, http://www1.cpdl.org/wiki/images/9/99/Bwv-ach1.pdf (accessed May 27, 2013).

30. Johann Sebastian Bach, *Alle Menschen Müssen Sterben*, BWV 262, edited by Claudio Macchi, http://www0.cpdl.org/wiki/images/7/7e/Bwv-allm.pdf (accessed May 27, 2013).

# 7

# METACOGNITION FOR INDEPENDENT MUSIC-PRACTICE SESSIONS

Independent practice is crucial for music learning. The combination of content knowledge, motor skill, and sensitivity to musical sound that facilitates rewarding music making is not achieved quickly or easily. Attending classes, rehearsals, and lessons is only the beginning of a music student's quest. Much of the learning and skill acquisition necessary for making progress in music are achieved during independent practice sessions. Metacognitive skills are central to effective and efficient practice. For musicians of any age who want to practice more effectively, Barry and Hallam offer the following suggestion: "Engage in metacognition—become mindful about practicing and related physical and mental processes. Be consciously aware of your own thought processes."[1]

Independent practice is self-teaching.[2] As such, it requires metacognition and self-regulation to meet the ongoing need for responding to encountered problems. Lehmann and Davidson have advised that "since this requires metacognitive or monitoring skills on the part of the musician, learning to practice is in itself a skill that needs to be acquired."[3]

Time spent practicing does not always ensure successful outcomes. Many novice music students practice by simply playing through entire pieces in a repetitive manner. They do not detect errors and stop to correct them. In fact, a counterproductive effect might occur as beginners

---

**Tips for Teachers**

Ask your students to explain to you *how* they go about practicing at home. Gaining insight into students' habitual practice procedures allows teachers to understand when it is necessary to make suggestions and to teach specific practice strategies.

---

reinforce errors by practicing them into the music. When they do pause for error correction, beginners tend to simply repeat individual notes in a type of musical stuttering. For many novice music students, practicing is not enjoyable or effective. It becomes a burdensome task, and the necessity to practice sometimes becomes a point of contention between parents and children. Teachers and parents cannot assure that students engage in deliberate, effective practice, as the amount of time spent in a session does not guarantee that the practicing is beneficial. Only the individual student can control the amount of deliberate practice that actually takes place during a practice session, and students can be successful only if they are taught *how* to practice effectively.[4]

## THE NATURE OF DELIBERATE AND EFFECTIVE MUSIC PRACTICE

Deliberate practice is defined as goal-oriented, structured, purposeful, and effortful practice.[5] It is viewed as taking place in three stages, as follows[6]:

1. *Phase 1: Planning and setting goals.* Metacognitive music learners set musical goals for each practice session. To do this, they use self-awareness and metacognitive declarative knowledge about their current strengths and weaknesses, what they already know and can do, and what they want to know and be able to do. Productive goals are both challenging and achievable. Successful music learners are able to distinguish between goals that can be accomplished in the current practice session and goals that will require extended practice over a longer period of time. As

metacognitive learners set goals for making progress in building performance skills, they also make realistic plans for what they will do in practice sessions to achieve those goals.

2. *Phase 2: Implementing plans with self-monitoring.* As music learners put plans into action, they use metacognitive procedural knowledge to apply strategies for achieving their goals. Additionally, music learners use metacognitive conditional knowledge to recognize when and why to apply goal-oriented strategies. (Strategy use is the most notable feature of practice among successful music students and expert musicians, and it will be explored later in this chapter). During this phase, music learners must apply self-awareness to monitor their own progress. A self-regulatory cycle proceeds, involving personal feedback and activity focused on improving performance.

   In order to self-monitor, music learners must have clear mental or aural representations of how the music should sound. Although repetitive drill may result in technical proficiency over time, it is through awareness of mental and aural representations that musicians are able to perform with expression and musicality. As they engage in problem solving in response to difficulties encountered in the music, metacognitive learners keep in mind both their goals and their mental and aural representations of the music.

3. *Phase 3: Self-evaluation.* As metacognitive music learners proceed through their practice sessions, they note their relative positions along a continuum of accomplishment from first reading to performance readiness for each piece in their repertoires. Self-evaluation helps learners to determine where they need help from a teacher, as well as what their future practice goals will be.

## Self-Regulation for Independent Music Practice

McPherson, Zimmerman, and Barry proposed three types of self-regulation that are applicable for music learning in independent practice.[7]

1. *Behavioral self-regulation* involves self-reflection and consequent adjustment of learning processes or methods to reach established goals. For example, an instrumentalist might decide to practice a

---

**Tips for Teachers**

Emphasize the 3-phase approach to independent practicing for your students.

- Goal-Setting. Students can set their own goals for every practice session.
- Monitoring. Students can monitor their own progress during every practice session.
- Evaluating. Students can evaluate their own progress at the end of every practice session.

Ask students to describe for you how they accomplish these steps in their at-home practice.

---

    section of music at a very slow tempo when technical difficulties must be resolved before playing up to tempo.
2. *Environmental self-regulation* involves observation and manipulation of the music-learning environment. For example, a young, self-regulating music learner will remove himself from family activities and close the door to his room when he is preparing to practice the clarinet.
3. *Covert self-regulation* involves monitoring, evaluating, and adjusting one's own thought processes for optimal music learning. For example, a pianist who finds her mind wandering during independent practice might begin to count rhythms out loud to bring her attention back to the task at hand.

## Metacognition in Expert Musicians

    As stated in chapter 3, metacognition and self-regulation are inextricably linked, and self-regulation is crucial for making progress in music. More than in academic subject areas, music students must make the choice to participate and are likely to drop out when bored or frustrated by a lack of positive outcomes. The use of productive practice habits contributes to students' retention in music-learning programs and their tenacious, ongoing progress toward expertise. For this reason, it is helpful to examine the practice habits of advanced students and expert musicians, as opposed to those of novices.

Expert musicians use metacognition to a greater extent than do novice musicians. Expert musicians' use of metacognition includes the following thoughts and actions:[8]

1. Reflective awareness of process and progress toward a defined goal
2. Awareness of task requirements
3. Identification of difficult passages in the music
4. Selection and implementation of appropriate cognitive and physical strategies for solving difficulties
5. Structuring of practice time for maximum effectiveness

Perhaps if novice music students are taught to use metacognition in their independent practice, their practice habits will begin to mimic those of expert musicians. In this way, perhaps novice music students can avoid the boredom and frustration that lead to attrition from music-education programs.

**Photo 7.1.   Third Grade Recorder Players**

## OVERVIEW OF RESEARCH ON
## INDEPENDENT MUSIC PRACTICE

### 1988—In a Study of the Practice Habits of Piano Students, Increased Strategy Use during Practice Appeared to Emerge as a By-product of Advancing Musicianship.

Linda Gruson studied strategy use among a group of pianists including young beginners, advanced students, and professional performers, comparing their uses of strategies during practice sessions. She found that as students advanced in musical expertise, their repertoire of practice strategies became increasingly larger and more cognitively complex. Gruson observed a shift from controlled processing to automaticity as students gained expertise through hours of deliberate practice.[9] According to Gruson, the shift occurred in this way:

> Musical practicing may be viewed as a sequence of transitions from controlled to automatic processing in which larger and larger chunks of musical information are built up from more-basic subcomponents. The novice student might be expected to focus [on] associating individual notes in the printed score with the corresponding positions on the musical instrument by means of controlled processing. With practice, the associations between printed notes and manual positions become automatized and attention may be focused [on] more complex musical patterns such as chords, measures, and ultimately phrases and larger units, which may, in turn come to be executed automatically from a single glance at the score.[10]

### 1992—In an Experimental Study, Nancy Barry Found that Structured and Strategic Practice Enabled Students to Achieve High Scores on Performance Tests.

According to Barry, "a highly organized and systematic regimen of supervised practice incorporating slow rehearsal, mental practice, distributed practice, and goal setting is an efficient and effective means of improving musical performance."[11] Barry conducted a study among fifty-five brass and woodwind players in grades 7 through 10. One group of students was assigned to practice independently for a specified amount of time under the supervision of adult monitors and with a structured agenda of practice strategies for each session. A second group of students was assigned to practice independently for the same amount of time, but these students were unsupervised and free to structure their own practice sessions. Barry found that those students who engaged in structured practice rich in practice strategies were able to attain higher scores on performance posttests in three areas: (1) melodic accuracy, (2) rhythmic accuracy, and (3) musicality.[12]

## 1994—Researchers Surveyed Music Teachers Regarding Instructions for Students' At-Home Practice.

Barry and McArthur investigated the extent to which applied-music teachers actively teach practice strategies to their students. They surveyed ninety-eight applied-music teachers, most of whom were piano teachers. The researchers found that most of the teachers reported always or almost always discussing practice strategies with their students during lessons.[13]

## 1994—In an Investigative Study, Researchers Found that Instrumental-Music Students Who Engaged in "Mindfulness" during Independent Practice Were More Likely to Apply Strategies for Developing Musicality as Well as Technical Proficiency in Their Playing.

Mindfulness in learning is exemplified by strategic behaviors, a sense of purpose, self-regulation, and conscious effort. Learning and practicing new music from notation both involve complex deciphering of a musical score, requiring a "concept of learning that embraces reflective or 'mindful' planning and processing."[14]

Cantwell and Millard conducted a study among eighth-grade instrumental-music students. The students were classified as either deep learners or surface learners according to their responses to Biggs's learning-process questionnaire. Surface learners were identified as those who tended to learn by rote, with little strategy use and notable dependence on a teacher or other outside influence. Conversely, deep learners demonstrated greater strategy use and less dependence on external help.[15] Cantwell and Millard found that when surface learners practiced music, they emphasized attainment of technical accuracy but did not go beyond technical considerations to matters of musical expression or interpretation. Surface learners used a restricted range of strategies consisting of rote learning and reliance on help from a teacher. Conversely, deep learners conceptualized technical accuracy in the broader context of musicality, focusing on expression and interpretation as well as the technical demands of the music.[16] Therefore, Cantwell and Millard advocated that music teachers should explicitly cue students to employ higher levels of processing when learning music. Furthermore, the researchers warned teachers that "the cuing of higher-level processing operations does not necessarily ensure transfer of these operations across tasks unless the interventions also incorporate explicit metacognitive components."[17] In other words, teachers have a responsibility to instruct students regarding the metacognitive skills of self-awareness, self-reflection, self-evaluation, and strategy use for independent music practice.

It should be noted that a current search of John Biggs's website reveals that Biggs now discourages educators from using his learning-process questionnaire for labeling students as deep learners or surface learners. Instead, Biggs encourages use of the questionnaire as a means of assessing teaching.[18] Noting that students adopt deep- or surface-learning approaches in response to different types of learning tasks, Biggs asserts that "it is therefore quite inappropriate to categorise students as 'surface' or 'deep' learners on the basis of SPQ responses, as if an approach score measured a stable trait of the individual. SPQ responses are a function of *both* individual characteristics *and* the teaching context. Both teacher and student are jointly responsible for the outcome, the teacher for structuring the enabling conditions, the learner for engaging them. Thus, an approach to learning describes the nature of the relationship between student, context, and task."[19]

## 1996—Researchers Investigated the Practice Habits of 257 Instrumental-Music Students.[20]

Deliberate, formal practice is necessary to making progress in building music-performance skills. In a study of practice habits among instrumental-music students between the ages of eight and eighteen, Sloboda, Davidson, Howe, and Moore found a direct relationship between the amount of deliberate practice and the achievement of music-performance goals.[21] They defined *deliberate practice* as effortful and structured, marked by a high degree of self-monitoring and strategy use for overcoming problems or weaknesses. Although the researchers found that deliberate, formal practice is required for achievement of technical goals, they also suggested that informal, playful engagement in improvisatory and exploratory music making might have a positive effect on development of musical expression.[22]

## 1997—In an Investigative Study, Susan Hallam Compared the Practice Habits of Expert and Novice Musicians.

Regarding independent music practice, Hallam stated that "the musician requires considerable metacognitive skills in relation to the task to be completed and for supporting practice—for example, managing time, maintaining concentration, maintaining motivation."[23] She noted that "practice is essentially a problem-solving activity"[24] requiring continuous self-evaluation. According to Hallam, *effective* music practice is "that which achieves the desired end product, in as short a time as possible, without interfering negatively with longer-term goals."[25]

Hallam investigated the components of effective practice by examining the practice habits of expert or professional musicians and comparing them with those of novice musicians (students). In Hallam's study, metacognition emerged as a central characteristic of the practice habits of professional musicians. She found that although expert musicians showed differences in preferred approaches to practice, they all demonstrated strong metacognitive skills, including planning, self-monitoring, and strategic decision making. Hallam noted that "all of the [professional] musicians exhibited considerable metacognitive skills. They were aware of their own strengths and weaknesses and the demands that various tasks made on them and had developed a range of practising strategies to optimize performance."[26]

Conversely, Hallam found that the children in her study did not have knowledge of music-practicing strategies and did not use metacognition spontaneously, as expert musicians did. This result led Hallam to advocate that teachers should view practicing as self-teaching and therefore provide their students with instruction in metacognitive reflection for learning how to learn during independent practice. Hallam also found that as students developed expertise in music, their strategy use increased along with their ability to plan and organize independent practice sessions. Apparently, as student musicians mature, an increased use of metacognition accompanies their increased levels of expertise.[27]

## 1997—Gary McPherson Investigated Instrumental-Music Students' Use of Strategies and Metacognitive Skills in Independent Practice.

Independent practice is enhanced when music students apply the metacognitive skills of monitoring and controlling their thought processes. In follow-up research to a longitudinal study of junior high and high school instrumental students' skill acquisition, McPherson sought to "explore the relationship between subjects' reported cognitive strategies used to perform in each style of musical performance and actual skill as evaluated on each of the measures."[28] The researcher interviewed the students, asking them to explain their thought processes as they prepared to play tests of three musical skills: (1) playing by ear, (2) playing from memory, and (3) improvising.[29] McPherson found that "the best musicians on each of the measures possessed a rich repertoire of strategies, which they used when preparing to perform. For example, comments by the clarinetist who received the highest score . . . display a mature level of metacognitive ability." Conversely, McPherson found that students who displayed the weakest performance skills were those who displayed the least ability to use metacognitive self-monitoring and control during practice and performance. Therefore, they were less able than their peers to detect and solve problems as they practiced.[30]

## 1999—McPherson and McCormick Found that "Harder-Working Musicians Tend to Report Higher Levels of Cognitive-Strategy Use."[31]

In a study conducted among 190 college pianists engaged in practicing for a performance examination, McPherson and McCormick found that higher-achieving students used cognitive strategies to a greater degree than their less-successful peers. Higher-achieving students were more likely to engage in mental rehearsing and to use self-evaluation for organizing their practice sessions efficiently, giving more time and attention to aspects of their music that needed more work. According to the researchers, "it may be that students who are more cognitively engaged while practicing not only tend to do more practice but are also more efficient with their learning."[32]

## 1999—In a Case Study, Siw Nielsen Found that Advanced Organ Students Exhibited a High Degree of Strategy use During Practice.

According to Nielsen, successful students tend to plan their learning and "spontaneously invent strategies" to improve performance.[33] Nielsen defined *strategies* as systematic activities, originally consciously applied, that become increasingly automatic as students gain expertise. Furthermore, he asserted that strategies are goal-directed activities that involve both cognition and action. Based on results of the case study, Nielsen advocated that music teachers should instruct their students in strategy use for independent practice.[34]

## 2000—In a Longitudinal Study of 158 Band Students, Pitts, Davidson, and McPherson Investigated the Practice Habits of Children Who Were Beginning Brass and Woodwind Players.

Practicing independently between lessons or classes requires self-monitoring. Music learners must remember their teachers' instructions and use that information for self-evaluation during independent practice sessions. In a study of the practice habits of beginning instrumentalists, Pitts, Davidson, and McPherson found that beginners showed little or no strategy use. They played through pieces without self-correcting. The researchers noted that repetition alone is insufficient to developing musicianship. Repetition with direction and purpose to correct specific problems will, however, bring about positive results.[35]

Beginning instrumentalists may not be able to recognize and correct mistakes in their playing because they must preoccupy themselves with handling their instruments and with fingerings, embouchure, and breath control. The researchers found that beginning instrumentalists engaged in more-productive practice sessions when they were able to remember and apply the practice strategies taught to them by their teachers. This conclusion led them to advise music teachers to spend time explaining and modeling practice strategies for their students while simultaneously placing on students the responsibility for identifying problem areas that require strategic attention. Furthermore, they advocated that to avoid the relatively nonproductive routine of continuous, rote repetition, teachers should encourage students to enrich their practice sessions by experimenting with dynamics and tempi during warm-up exercises and to occasionally return to previously learned repertoire to build confidence by enjoying ease and fluency in playing.[36] Regarding independent practice, Pitts, Davidson, and McPherson suggested that "making progress on the instrument should not be seen as the only practice goal: musical understanding and cognitive processing must also be allowed to develop so that learning can be independent and ongoing."[37]

## 2001—Susan Hallam Investigated the Relationships between Strategy Use and Development of Expertise among Beginning and Advanced Music Students.

Hallam conducted a study of strategy use among fifty-five strings players, ages six to eighteen, ranging from beginners to advanced players.[38] Sixty percent of students in Hallam's study left errors uncorrected during their practice sessions. Additionally, they reinforced errors by practicing them into their performances of repertoire.[39]

Hallam found that the metacognitive skill of planning for learning is beneficial for students engaged in independent practice. Table 7.1 shows the results of Hallam's study regarding the importance of planning in practice sessions as it relates to students' musical advancement.[40]

Based on the results, Hallam concluded that "the effective use of practicing strategies depends to some extent on the development of expertise. If students do not have sufficient musical knowledge, having knowledge of effective practicing strategies will be of limited use. Effective practice depends on the learner having metacognitive and musical knowledge."[41]

**Table 7.1. Results of Hallam's Study**

| | |
|---|---|
| High level of planning in practice sessions characterized by:<br>(1) evidence of completion of task requirements<br>(2) speedy identification of difficulties<br>(3) concentration of effort on difficult sections<br>(4) integration of sections practiced into whole for<br>performance | 12.5% of novice students<br><br>100% of advanced students |
| Moderate level of planning in practice sessions as<br>characterized by:<br>(1) completion of task requirements<br>(2) evidence of on-task behavior but repetition of large<br>sections of work rather than a focus on difficulties<br>(3) no integration specifically toward performance | 70% of novice students |
| Low level of planning in practice sessions as characterized by:<br>(1) task not completed<br>(2) first part of music practiced, but not the remainder<br>(3) considerable amounts of time spent off-task | 17.5% of novice students |

## 2001—In a Longitudinal Study, Researchers Found that Some Beginning Music Students Did Use Practice Strategies Similar to Those of More Advanced Musicians.

McPherson and Renwick conducted an investigative study in which seven children, ages seven to nine (at the beginning of the treatment period), videotaped their practice sessions at home over a period of three years. The researchers found low levels of metacognitive monitoring and control, as evidenced by self-regulatory behavior. Most students employed a limited strategy of playing through pieces, ignoring errors, or making slight adjustments to one or two notes.[42]

McPherson and Renwick also found that some students did self-regulate better than others, beginning in early stages of music study. Interestingly, some beginners demonstrated processes that were similar to those of expert musicians, even when their level of musical expertise was far from advanced. The researchers concluded that "self-regulatory processes are used to greater or lesser degrees in young musicians. Most importantly, our results indicate that these differences emerge from the very first practice session and that they account for a large part of a student's subsequent progress."[43]

McPherson and Renwick made a strong case for music teachers promoting self-reflection and metacognitive control among their students. They provided the following suggestions for music teachers:

> Teachers should spend time during their lessons demonstrating and modeling specific strategies that their students can try when practicing, such as how to correct or prevent certain types of performance errors. However, such strategies will be ineffective unless the learners also develop their capacity to monitor and control their own learning. Consequently, teachers should also devise strategies whereby learners can be encouraged to reflect on the adequacy of their own practice habits, and especially on how they might invent better ways (such as self-reflective comments in their diaries) that will help them practice more efficiently. Our preliminary findings suggest that the skills of knowing how to self-monitor, set goals, and use appropriate strategies take time to develop in most young children. Helping beginning instrumentalists to reflect on their own progress and ability to employ self-regulatory processes may go some way to improving instrumental instruction, especially for children who do not pick up these skills informally.[44]

## 2006—Researchers Found that Some Music Students Approached Practicing Analytically, While Others Adopted a Holistic Approach.

Rohwer and Polk studied the practice behaviors of sixty-five eighth-grade instrumental students. They identified students in four categories with regard to practice habits. About half of their participants were classified in holistic categories, and half were classified in analytic categories.[45] Rohwer and Polk found the following results:

1. *Holistic, noncorrective practicers* tended to simply play through pieces without stopping to correct errors. These students received the lowest scores on performance tests.
2. *Holistic, corrective practicers* consistently played through pieces, but they did stop momentarily to correct errors. These students received the next-lowest scores on performance tests.
3. *Analytic, reactive practicers* also tended to practice pieces sequentially (from beginning to end), but they frequently stopped to

give extended attention to difficult passages, isolating sections and correcting mistakes within the linear context of playing through their pieces. These students received the highest scores on performance tests.

4. *Analytic, proactive practicers* tended not to start at the beginning of their pieces. Instead, they immediately jumped to the most difficult sections. They gave attention to correcting errors, but not within the linear context of playing through pieces. These students received the second-highest scores on performance tests.

In summary, the analytic practicers received significantly higher scores than the holistic practicers in the study, and those students who used analytic self-evaluation to correct mistakes within the linear context of playing through their pieces were the most successful on performance tests.[46]

Based on the results, Rohwer and Polk advocated that music teachers endeavor to teach analytic practicing to students. They suggested that teachers might use reflective modeling to teach students to detect errors and to devise strategies for correcting errors. For example, when stopping to correct an error, the teacher could first ask the students if they can identify the error. Then, the teacher can ask for students' input regarding a strategy to fix the error. In this way, the teacher models the type of thought process that students will need for effective independent practice.[47] It is evident that analytic practicing requires metacognition through self-reflection and self-evaluation on the part of the students.

## 2008—Based on Results of a Case Study, Margaret Berg Advocated that Teachers Should Differentiate Instruction to Meet Specific Needs of Their Individual Students.

In a study of the practice habits of two seventh-grade female strings players in their third year of instruction, Berg found differing levels of strategy application in practice sessions, despite identical ages, gender, and years of study.[48] Based on results, Berg advocated that teachers should develop and model differentiated practice strategies for their students. This differentiation could be based on questionnaires whereby teachers solicit information from students regarding their preferred practice routines and their knowledge of varied practice strategies. Furthermore, Berg advised that teachers should require their students to keep practice records that contain not only time spent but also practice routines, strategies, notes on difficulties, and steps taken to correct problems.[49] Practice records that are rich in specific information might help teachers to develop differentiated instruction based on students' individual needs.

## 2008—Based on a Study Conducted Among College Music Students, Researchers Emphasized the Importance of Metacognition in Independent Practice.

In an investigative study of practice habits, Byo and Cassidy found that college music majors identified "better self-discipline" as the one factor that would most likely improve effectiveness of their independent practice sessions.[50] The researchers referred to deliberate practice, noting that quantity does not always equate to quality in practicing. Byo and Cassidy observed that strategic behaviors, such as slowing down and repeating difficult passages, were "little more than inert activities" if metacognition was not involved.[51] Some participants in their study used strategies optimally, and others did not. Byo and Cassidy acknowledged the strong influence of metacognition on effective, deliberate practice:

> Practice is also structured on the basis of metacognitive skill. Metacognition was demonstrated by musicians who were aware of personal skill level, the nature and difficulty of targeted performance behaviors, appropriate practice strategies, and personal concentration level. Practice was dominated by self-evaluation, which served as a prompt for the practicer to adapt procedures according to need. Self-regulation, a similar construct, is characterized by a cyclic process of self-monitoring, self-evaluating, and adaptive behavior in the learner's ongoing pursuit of a goal. Metacognition and self-regulation acknowledge the conditional, not fixed, nature of practice and are evident in the practice of advanced and novice performers.[52]

## 2009—In an Investigative Study of Practice Behaviors, Strategy Use for Correcting Errors (Rather than Amount of Time Spent Practicing) Emerged as the Greatest Predictor of Success.

In a study of advanced undergraduate and graduate piano majors, Duke, Simmons, and Cash found that a higher level of strategy use characterized the practice habits of students who demonstrated greater success in performance quality and retention of learning.[53] The researchers found that the most notable differences between top-scoring pianists and those who were less successful emerged in the area of handling errors. Top-ranked pianists were better able to detect and correct errors during practice. The researchers, therefore, advocated that music teachers should teach students about error detection and correction. They asserted that developing the ability to detect and correct errors is more important than filling a prescribed number of minutes with practice every day.[54]

## 2012—In an Intervention Study, Researchers Found that Music Teachers had a Significant Impact on Whether their Students Realized Greater Gains Through Use of Metacognitive Skills during Independent Practice.

Bathgate, Sims-Knight, and Schunn conducted a study in which applied-music teachers were given training in how to promote metacognition among their students.[55] Prior to the training, teachers may have taught metacognitive skills to some degree, but preliminary results indicated that their students were not using metacognition to a great extent. Final results indicated that when teachers understood metacognition and explicitly encouraged its use among their students for independent practice, students' scores on music-performance tests increased significantly. Additionally, when music teachers explicitly taught metacognitive skills, their novice students developed reflective and process-oriented approaches to practice, similar to approaches that are normally observed among expert musicians. The researchers noted that beneficial results from applications of metacognition in practice sessions were achieved without increasing the amount of time spent in practice.[56]

## 2012—In a Qualitative Study, Steve Oare Explored Effective Practice Habits of Young Instrumentalists.

In a study conducted among five junior high school band students, Oare found that goal setting, strategy use, and self-evaluation were components of effective practice. Less experienced students appeared to focus their practice sessions on filling a requisite amount of playing time. More experienced students took an analytic approach whereby they selected difficult spots in the music for repetitive practice.[57]

Oare recommended that students set their own practice goals and that those goals be (1) specific, (2) short term (accomplished within the practice session), and (3) moderately challenging but not so difficult that achievement is out of reach.[58] Additionally, Oare delineated three factors that he found to be important in strategy use during practice:

1. Students need a repertoire of strategies. They may develop some of their strategies for themselves, or they may use strategies taught by their teacher.
2. Students need to know when and how to apply known strategies in practice.
3. Students must be motivated to apply strategies.

In order to implement these factors, students must have metacognitive knowledge, including declarative knowledge of strengths and weaknesses to recognize the need for strategy use, procedural knowledge to know how to practice, and conditional knowledge to understand when, why, and how to apply practice strategies for achievement of specific performance goals.

In addition to goal setting and strategy use, Oare emphasized the importance of self-evaluation in deliberate practice. He delineated three factors that influenced students' abilities to self-evaluate:

1. Students must have a clear idea of what a successful performance of the piece sounds like, and, more importantly, they should be able to explain the criteria of a successful performance.
2. Students must develop self-awareness for error detection and correction.
3. Once students recognize mistakes, they must engage in self-reflection to diagnose the causes of mistakes.[59]

Oare concluded that focusing on time spent in practice is less advantageous that focusing on musical goals. For this reason, he advised teachers to require documentation of students' goal setting and self-evaluations in their practice logs. Oare advocated grading of practice logs based in part on students self-monitoring their progress toward performance goals on a daily or weekly basis.

## METACOGNITION AND STRATEGY USE IN INDEPENDENT PRACTICE

Metacognition appears to develop in young musicians along two planes. As they acquire maturity and experience, music learners acquire declarative metacognitive knowledge regarding what they know and can do and what they need to know and want to be able to do. Simultaneously, they develop procedural and conditional metacognitive knowledge as they build a repertoire of practice strategies that they can apply to solving problems and accomplishing their music-performance goals.

Numerous researchers emphasize strategy use as the predominant factor in developing advanced or expert music-performance skill, and metacognition lies at the core of strategic behavior. Researchers define the term *strategies* in various ways. A sampling of these definitions includes:

- "skill made deliberate."[60]
- "behaviors and thoughts in which a learner engages and which are intended to influence the learner's encoding process."[61]
- processes that are purposeful and directed toward a goal of improved performance.[62]
- goal-directed activities that involve both cognition and action.[63]

### Recommended Practice Strategies

Throughout the literature on independent music practice, researchers cite many specific strategies. These strategies are identified as processes that facilitate positive outcomes for novice and expert musicians, thereby optimizing the time and effort spent in practice sessions. The following list of practice strategies is gleaned from research studies that have been referenced previously in this chapter. Researchers advocate use of the following strategies for developing expertise in music performance:

- Analyzing a new piece before playing it.
- Audio-recording practice sessions for playback and self-evaluation
- Aural processing.
- Building a mental representation that can be easily translated into sound.
- Cognitive processing.
- Counting rhythms aloud.
- Creating personal programs for psychomotor learning, such as motor exercises for fluency and accuracy in fingerings.
- Developing and using a desirable aural image of the music as a guide for self-evaluating and setting practice goals.
- Developing technique exercises based on the piece.
- Discriminating among performance targets: recognizing those that are achievable now and those that will require extended practice over a longer period of time.
- Distinguishing between two practice needs: the need for continuous play-through and the need for a stop-and-start protocol for problem solving, with repetition of technically demanding passages.
- Dividing a piece into large working sections that are focused separately.
- Engaging in assigned listening activities as a part of practice.
- Experimenting with alternate solutions to a problem.
- Following a written practice format provided by the teacher.
- Goal setting—setting achievable and specific goals for each practice session.
- Identifying the difficult passages of a piece: marking errors and practicing those sections very slowly.
- Identifying and selecting specific performance targets.
- Identifying similarities and dissimilarities in the music.
- Immediately identifying errors.
- Immediately correcting errors when they appear in the practice session and practicing problematic passages adequately so that mistakes are not repeated.

- Isolating difficult sections of a piece for special attention.
- Keeping a practice record, although merely recording time spent does not ensure effective practice. It may be helpful to record goals, strategies, strengths and weaknesses, and difficulties encountered in the music; as well as hours and minutes spent in practicing.
- Keeping only one fingering, making it the same every time.
- Letting the body rest briefly when needed.
- Maintaining flexibility in practice rather than an overly strict adherence to a fixed regimen.
- Manipulating the size of a section to be practiced in response to difficulties encountered.
- Mapping—playing through a piece to identify problem spots.
- Marking the music—key signature, meter signature, accidentals, terms and definitions, places where errors occur.
- Memorization techniques.
- Mentally rehearsing a piece before playing it.
- Metronome—using a metronome consistently and systematically throughout practice.
- Minimizing patterns of movements or purposefully exaggerating movements to achieve technique goals.
- Pausing during practice to study the score further.
- Performing relaxation exercises when needed.
- Playing hands separately (keyboard players) and hands/pedals separately (organists).
- Playing sections of a piece in different tempi.
- Playing sections of music along with verbalization, such as counting aloud or singing melodic intervals.
- Practice distribution—when possible, having two short practice sessions per day rather than one long session.
- Practice tempo—starting slowly and gradually increasing the tempo.
- Practicing as if in performance with an audience listening.
- Practicing difficult passages out of context.
- Practicing the most difficult pieces early in the session.
- Practicing the pieces that need the most work.
- Practicing with inflection in early stages of learning a piece.

- Preparing the body and muscles for a practice session.
- Purposefully altering the rhythm patterns of a section to overcome technical problems.
- Purposefully repeating larger sections or entire pieces.
- Purposefully repeating small sections or single measures.
- Repetitive drilling of sections in a piece of music.
- Repetitive practicing at a slow tempo.
- Researching and listening to recordings of a piece.
- Responding to perceptual feedback.
- Self-evaluating continuously, based on aural and physical feedback.
- Self-talk for self-teaching and working out problems.
- Silent practice—examining the music before playing—practicing fingering silently before playing.
- Simplifying a challenging passage.
- Simplifying technical problems by temporarily ignoring the rhythm.
- Singing the music in your head while practicing.
- Singing/humming the part (for instrumentalists).
- Supervised practice—practice sessions supervised by an adult.
- Tapping rhythm patterns.
- Tempo variations—slowing down and speeding up.
- Using a whole-part-whole approach—the student plays through a piece, breaks it down into small sections for repetitive practice, and then puts small sections back into context of the whole piece.
- Using combinations of strategies in sequence.
- Verbalizations—reading note names aloud, counting aloud, giving self-instructions aloud.

The list of practice strategies gleaned from research studies referenced in this chapter is quite extensive. Some of the strategies appear to be most suited to children or beginners, while others might be used by advanced students or expert musicians. Music educators reading this chapter might think of other practice strategies to add to the list. Music students might devise their own strategies for solving problems encountered in practice sessions. When music teachers share strategic information with their students and encourage them to devise their own practice strategies, teachers help students to develop self-regulation for independent learning.

## Applying Practice Strategies for Music Learning

Metacognition is needed for intelligent application of strategies in independent practice. Typically, novice music students learn practice strategies from their teachers, but when strategies are applied without metacognition, the result is mindless drill.[64] This type of practicing produces, at best, a mediocre performance, absent the kind of expressive interpretation that emanates from deep musical understanding. As students make progress in music, it might be necessary to discard practice strategies that are intended for beginners and to replace them with more advanced strategies for continued growth. For example, rote imitation and rote memorization may be effective for a beginner but should be replaced with musically expressive interpretation and score analysis by a more advanced student.[65]

One hallmark of effective practice is that it helps students to move from conscious application of strategies to automaticity. This shift from controlled to automatic processes requires metacognition. Learners must be aware of cognitive processes in order to execute control over them. As learners progress from conscious to automatic execution of music-making skills, they use *chunking*—that is, "combining several ideas or actions so that they are treated as a single unit in working memory."[66] Learners must achieve automaticity in order to free up the information-processing load so that new learning can take place, and "automaticity requires extensive practice."[67] For example, this phenomenon is observed in beginning instrumental students. At first, they are so preoccupied with handling their instruments and producing a tone that they have little awareness left over for listening to themselves and self-monitoring. As instrumentalists become more

---

### Tips for Teachers

Help students to build a repertoire of appropriate strategies for independent practice. Discuss practice strategies during music classes and one-to-one lessons. Demonstrate and suggest practice strategies for students. Ask students to create their own strategies and to evaluate their effectiveness.

advanced, their playing becomes more automatic, and they are able to focus on more complex cognitive and motor skills, along with more refined musical expression.

## TEACHING STUDENTS HOW TO PRACTICE

In all areas of education, teachers are called on to teach learning strategies to their students. It is not enough that teachers expect students to acquire assigned knowledge and skills. They must equip students for the job by teaching strategies that students can use to achieve their goals.[68] Educational researchers find that when instruction in metacognitive skills is embedded in course content, students are better able to regulate their own learning in self-directed learning situations.[69] This is true of music learning, as well as learning in academic disciplines.

The following list of suggestions is provided for teachers who want to teach their students how to practice:

- Assist students in developing desirable mental and aural representations of the music by providing an accurate model. This can be accomplished by playing or singing the music for students during instructional time or by directing students to listen to a good recording. Emphasize to students that a model of the music is not provided for the purpose of copying but, instead, for establishing a standard of excellence in performance.
- Use an individualized approach, when possible. Select and demonstrate appropriate strategies for solving specific problems that arise in the repertoire to be practiced. As the teacher demonstrates practice strategies during a lesson or class, students can build their own strategy arsenals and measure their understanding of how to go about practicing.
- During lessons or classes, when problems arise in difficult passages of music, encourage students to develop their own strategies for solving the problems. If the teacher refrains from immediately offering a solution but instead guides students to create their own solutions, the teacher helps students to develop metacognitive self-regulation, as necessary for independent practice.

- Instruct students to engage in enriching activities during independent-practice sessions such as listening, sight-reading, sightsinging, and directed improvisation.
- Require students to maintain and submit practice logs that include information about goal setting, practice strategies, and self-evaluation for each independent practice session. A template for such a practice log may be found in chapter 3.
- Encourage students to audio record themselves in practice sessions and to use the recordings for self-evaluation.
- Ask students to verbalize their practice goals before leaving a lesson or class. The teacher can emphasize that improved performance will be expected in the next lesson or class, based on the students' stated practice goals.

Teaching students to use metacognitive self-regulation in independent practice requires that teachers strike a balance between expecting too much and expecting too little. Beginning music students are generally not able to generate their own mental or aural representations of the music; nor are they able to devise their own practice strategies for achieving a successful performance of the music. For these reasons, teachers of beginning students find that it is necessary to spend more time and effort in providing accurate models and demonstrating specific practice strategies. As students become increasingly advanced in musicianship and performance skills, however, teachers might expect them to develop accurate mental or aural representations of the music and to devise their own strategies for solving encountered problems. With sensitivity to students' relative levels of advancement, it is always appropriate for teachers to expect music learners to use the metacognitive skills of planning, goal setting, self-awareness, self-monitoring, and self-evaluation during independent practice sessions.

## NOTES

1. Nancy H. Barry and Susan Hallam, "Practice," in *The Science and Psychology of Music Performance*, edited by Richard Parncutt and Gary E. McPherson (New York: Oxford University Press, 2002), 160.

2. Susan Hallam, "What Do We Know about Practicing? Towards a Model Synthesising the Research Literature," in *Does Practice Make Perfect? Current Theory and Research on Instrumental Music Practice*, edited by Harald Jørgensen and Andreas Lehmann (Oslo: Norges Musikkhøgskole, 1997), 180–81; Steve Oare, "Decisions Made in the Practice Room: A Qualitative Study of Middle School Students' Thought Processes while Practicing," *Update: Applications of Research in Music Education* 30, no. 2 (2012): 64.

3. Andreas C. Lehmann and Jane W. Davidson, "Taking an Acquired Skills Perspective on Music Performance," in *MENC Handbook of Musical Cognition and Development*, edited by Richard Colwell (New York: Oxford University Press, 2006), 243.

4. Nancy H. Barry, "The Effects of Practice Strategies, Individual Differences in Cognitive Style, and Gender upon Technical Accuracy and Musicality of Student Instrumental Performance," *Psychology of Music* 20 (1992): 121; Carl Bereiter and Marlene Scardamalia, "Cognition and Curriculum," in *Handbook of Research on Curriculum: A Project of the American Educational Research Association*, edited by Philip W. Jackson (New York: MacMillan, 1992), 530; Susan Hallam, "The Development of Expertise in Young Musicians: Strategy Use, Knowledge Acquisition and Individual Diversity," *Music Education Research* 3, no. 1 (2001): 9–10; Andreas C. Lehmann and K. Anders Ericsson, "Research on Expert Performance and Deliberate Practice: Implications for the Education of Amateur Musicians and Music Students," *Psychomusicology* 16, no. 1–2 (1997): 48; Gary E. McPherson and Barry J. Zimmerman, "Self-Regulation of Musical Learning: A Social Cognitive Perspective on Developing Performance Skills," in *MENC Handbook of Research on Music Learning, vol. 2: Applications*, edited by Richard Colwell and Peter R. Webster (New York: Oxford University Press, 2011), 132.

5. Hallam, "What Do We Know," 180; Lehmann and Ericsson, "Research on Expert Performance," 44; Gary E. McPherson and James M. Renwick, "A Longitudinal Study of Self-Regulation in Children's Musical Practice," *Music Education Research* 3, no. 2 (2001): 169.

6. Margaret H. Berg, "Getting the Minutes In: A Case Study of Beginning Instrumentalists' Music Practice," in *Diverse Methodologies in the Study of Music Teaching and Learning*, edited by Linda K. Thompson and Mark Robin Campbell (Charlotte, N.C.: Information Age Publishing, 2008), 46; Janet E. Davidson and Robert J. Sternberg, "Smart Problem Solving: How Metacognition Helps," in *Metacognition in Educational Theory and Practice*, edited by Douglas J. Hacker, John Dunlosky, and Arthur Graesser (Mahwah, N.J.: Lawrence Erlbaum Associates, 1998), 50; Hallam, "What Do We Know," 81; Lehmann and Ericsson, "Research on Expert Performance," 47–48; Scott G. Paris, Marjorie Y. Lipson, and

Karen K. Wixson, "Becoming a Strategic Reader," *Contemporary Educational Psychology* 8, no. 3 (1983): 293; Robert H. Woody, "Learning from the Experts: Applying Research in Expert Performance to Music Education," *Update: Applications of Research in Music Education* 19, no. 9 (2001): 11–12.

7. McPherson and Zimmerman, "Self-Regulation of Musical Learning," 131.

8. Meghan Bathgate, Judith Sims-Knight, and Christian Schunn, "Thoughts on Thinking: Engaging Novice Music Students in Metacognition," *Applied Cognitive Psychology* 26, no. 2 (2012): 403, doi:10.1002/acp.1842.

9. Linda M. Gruson, "Rehearsal Skill and Musical Competence: Does Practice Make Perfect?" in *Generative Processes in Music: The Psychology of Performance, Improvisation, and Composition*, edited by John A. Sloboda (New York: Oxford University Press, 1988), 106–107.

10. Ibid., 108.

11. Barry, "Effects of Practice Strategies," 121.

12. Ibid., 119.

13. Nancy H. Barry and Victoria McArthur, "Teaching Practice Strategies in the Music Studio: A Survey of Applied Music Teachers," *Psychology of Music* 22 (1994): 47.

14. Robert H. Cantwell and Yvette Millard, "The Relationship between Approach to Learning and Learning Strategies in Learning Music," *British Journal of Educational Psychology* 64, no. 1 (1994): 45.

15. Ibid., 50–51.

16. Ibid., 60–61.

17. Ibid., 61.

18. John Biggs, "Student Approaches to Learning," http://www.johnbiggs .com.au/academic/students-approaches-to-learning/ (accessed December 18, 2013), par. 3.

19. John Biggs, David Kember, and Doris Y. P. Leung, "The Revised Two Factor Study Process Questionnaire: R-SPQ-2F," *British Journal of Educational* Psychology 71 (2001): 5, 136–137, www.johnbiggs.com.au/students_ approaches.html (accessed January 16, 2013).

20. John A. Sloboda, Jane W. Davidson, Michael J. A. Howe, and Derek G. Moore, "The Role of Practice in the Development of Performing Musicians," *British Journal of Psychology* 87, no. 2 (1996): 291.

21. Ibid., 306.

22. Ibid., 289.

23. Susan Hallam, "Approaches to Instrumental Music Practice of Experts and Novices: Implications for Education," in *Does Practice Make Perfect? Current Theory and Research on Instrumental Music Practice*, edited by Harald Jørgensen and Andreas Lehmann (Oslo: Norges Musikkhøgskole, 1997), 91–92.

24. Ibid., 90.

25. Ibid., 91.

26. Ibid., 98.

27. Ibid., 103–104.

28. Gary E. McPherson, "Cognitive Strategies and Skill Acquisition in Musical Performance," *Bulletin of the Council for Research in Music Education*, no. 133 (Summer 1997): 65.

29. Ibid., 66.

30. Ibid., 70.

31. Gary E. McPherson and John McCormick, "Motivational and Self-Regulated Learning Components of Musical Practice," *Bulletin of the Council for Research in Music Education*, no. 141 (Summer 1999): 101.

32. Ibid.

33. Siw G. Nielsen, "Learning Strategies in Instrumental Music Practice," *British Journal of Music Education* 16, no. 3 (1999): 275.

34. Ibid., 289.

35. Stephanie Pitts, Jane Davidson, and Gary McPherson, "Developing Effective Practice Strategies: Case Studies of Three Young Instrumentalists," *Music Education Research* 2, no. 1 (2000): 46.

36. Ibid., 54.

37. Ibid., 55.

38. Hallam, "Development of Metacognition," 8.

39. Ibid., 10.

40. Ibid., 13.

41. Ibid., 15.

42. Gary E. McPherson and James M. Renwick, "A Longitudinal Study of Self-Regulation in Children's Musical Practice," *Music Education Research* 3, no. 2 (2001): 172–73.

43. Ibid., 184.

44. Ibid.

45. Debbie Rohwer and Jeremy Polk, "Practice Behaviors of Eighth-Grade Instrumental Musicians," *Journal of Research in Music Education* 54, no. 4 (2006): 355.

46. Ibid., 356–57.

47. Ibid., 360.

48. Berg, "Getting the Minutes In," 57.

49. Ibid., 61–62.

50. James L. Byo and Jane W. Cassidy, "An Exploratory Study of Time Use in the Practice of Music Majors: Self-Report and Observation Analysis," *Update: Applications of Research in Music Education* 27, no. 1. (2008): 33.

51. Ibid., 38.

52. Ibid., 34.

53. Robert A. Duke, Amy L. Simmons, and Carla D. Cash, "It's Not How Much; It's How," *Journal of Research in Music Education* 56, no. 4 (2009): 318.

54. Ibid., 319.

55. Bathgate, Sims-Knight, and Schunn, "Thoughts on Thinking," 404.

56. Ibid., 408.

57. Oare, "Decisions Made," 65.

58. Ibid., 67.

59. Ibid., 68.

60. Paris, Lipson, and Wixson, "Becoming a Strategic Reader," 296.

61. Claire E. Weinstein and Richard E. Mayer, "The Teaching of Learning Strategies," *Innovation Abstracts* 5, no. 32 (1983): 3, National Institute for Staff and Organizational Development.

62. Hallam, "What Do We Know," 200.

63. Nielsen, "Learning Strategies," 62.

64. Lehmann and Ericsson, "Research on Expert Performance," 48–49.

65. Ibid., 54–55.

66. Gruson, "Rehearsal Skill and Musical Competence," 529.

67. Ibid., 530.

68. Weinstein and Mayer, "Teaching of Learning Strategies," 1.

69. Joyce Kincannon, Conrad Gleber, and Jaehyun Kim, "The Effects of Metacognitive Training on Performance and Use of Metacognitive Skills in Self-Directed Learning Situations" (paper presented at the National Convention of the Association for Educational Communications and Technology, Houston, Tex., 1999, 173.

## 8

# WHAT CAN TEACHERS DO?

**T**he desire to impart independent, lifelong skills for music learning is a strong rationale for promoting metacognition among music learners. Teachers endeavor to promote metacognitive skills so that students will outgrow their dependence on teachers. As we have seen throughout this book, a wealth of pedagogical practices, emerging from research, allows music teachers to achieve this goal. Although some learners appear to use metacognition spontaneously and naturally, it is primarily the influence of teachers that allows students to develop self-awareness, goal-setting, planning, self-monitoring, strategy-use, reflection, and self-evaluation skills for music learning. In this final chapter, we will further explore teaching strategies designed to promote metacognition among music learners.

## EMBEDDING METACOGNITION IN MUSIC INSTRUCTION

It is likely that *no* music educator has ever uttered the following: "I have too much time in my music lessons, classes, and rehearsals. I cannot think of enough instructional procedures and activities to fill up all of the excess time that I have with my students." Generally, quite the opposite state of affairs exists in music classes, ensemble rehearsals, and one-to-one lessons. It seems that there is never enough time to cover everything. Because of time limitations, most instruction focuses on content rather than on learning strategies for acquiring content knowledge; however, encouraging students to reflect on learning need not take extra time. Exercising students' metacognitive skills can be embedded in direct instruction of content. Consequently, when student awareness of thinking is made known to the teacher, it can inform the teacher about necessary future directions for instruction.[1]

As stated previously in this book, it is *not* wise to conceptualize metacognition as a set of skills to be taught in discrete contexts outside the natural flow of discipline-specific instruction. Instead, music teachers can encourage students to use metacognitive skills within the contexts of lessons, rehearsals, music classes, composition projects, independent practice, listening, and performance experiences. Teachers might consider metacognitive skills to be tools for students to use while learning within the music discipline. It is important for teachers to remember that the capacity for metacognitive thought appears to develop in learners as they gain expertise in music. Students need to learn the *what* and *how* of music concurrently with developing metacognition for music learning. Susan Hallam provided the following list of topics that music teachers might discuss with their students.

- Personal strengths and weaknesses
- Assessing task difficulties
- Selecting appropriate practice strategies
- Setting goals and monitoring progress
- Evaluating performance
- Developing interpretation
- Strategies for memorization
- Enhancing motivation
- Time management
- Improving concentration
- Performance strategies[2]

**Photo 8.1. Vocal Exercises**

## QUESTIONING: A TOOL FOR TEACHERS

Metacognition is closely associated with higher-order-thinking skills; therefore, it is helpful to examine questioning techniques that have been shown to elicit higher-order thinking from students. Teachers can use carefully phrased questions to encourage students to reveal their thought processes. In their questions, teachers give cues to students regarding the depth of mental processes needed to answer the questions. Consequently, there is a direct relationship between the types of questions that teachers ask and the depth of thinking required of students.[3]

For example, a music teacher can ask a question that elicits a demonstration of content knowledge from students. After distributing a new piece of music in class, the teacher might ask, "Who can tell me what key this piece is in?" On the other hand, the teacher might ask a question that requires students to explain their thought processes: the teacher might say, "I see four flats in this key signature. Who can tell me how to figure out what major key or what relative-minor key this piece might be in?"

To answer the first question, students will respond with a factual bit of information that will be right or wrong. If one student in the class answers correctly, the teacher will likely move on, and other students may or may not know *why* the answer was correct. To answer the second question, students will need to explain their thought processes for determining tonality from a key signature. The information in the response will be richer and more in-depth; therefore, the teacher will have an enriched teaching opportunity to ensure that all of the students in the class understand an important process for music reading.

## Teachers' Responses

In addition to asking carefully phrased questions, teachers can promote learners' thinking skills through their responses to students' answers. Teachers might give closed responses or open, extending responses. Closed responses might be negative ("No, that's not right") or positive ("Yes, good job"). Either way, closed responses do not extend learning. On the other hand, open responses are designed to extend students' thinking and learning.[4] The following list describes several types of open, extending responses.

1. *Silence.* When teachers use wait time after asking a question, it gives students time to do their own reflecting and problem solving. Teachers sometimes think that they must fill every second with talking and instructions, but this is not always beneficial. Leaving some silence in a Q & A discussion session gives students time to think about their teachers' questions and about answers given by their peers.[5]

2. *Acceptance.* When students answer teachers' questions, it is helpful for teachers to show acceptance of their answers. Accepting responses helps to create a safe environment in which students are willing to share their thoughts. Even if students give incorrect answers, teachers can show acceptance and then proceed to help students understand the thought processes that lead to correct answers.[6]

3. *Clarifying and presenting information.* After showing acceptance of students' answers, teachers can redirect students' thinking by asking them to clarify their answers. After hearing students' clarifications, teachers might decide if they need to reteach concepts or present new information for students to form new concepts.[7]

Let us return to our previous example of a music teacher asking about the key signature and tonality of a new piece. Here is one possible scenario.

TEACHER: Who can tell me what key this piece is in? [*The question elicits a simple, factual response.*]

STUDENT: E-flat.

TEACHER: No. Who can tell me? [*The teacher gives a closed response and asks the question again.*]

SECOND STUDENT: A-flat.

TEACHER: Right. [*Teacher gives a closed response and moves on.*]

A different scenario might be as follows:

TEACHER: I see four flats in this key signature. Who can tell me how to figure out what major key or what relative-minor key this piece might be in? [*The question elicits information about thought processes.*]

STUDENT: Well, I usually read the flats from left to right and notice the next-to-last flat because it is the name of the key. So, this piece is in A-flat. [*The student explains their personal thought processes and gives a partial answer to the teacher's question.*]

TEACHER: You are thinking about it correctly, and you could be right. But what if it is in a minor key? What minor key might it be? [*The teacher shows acceptance and extends thinking.*]

SECOND STUDENT: I think it might be F minor, because F is the sixth step in the A-flat major scale. That makes it the relative minor. [*The student explains their personal thought processes and completes the answer to the teacher's question.*]

TEACHER: And you are thinking about it correctly, too. So, you also got the right answer. Does everybody understand how they got the right answers? [*The teacher shows acceptance and checks for understanding among other students in the class.*]

In the second scenario, the teacher requires that the student explain their thought processes and extend their thinking. The resulting socially shared metacognition benefits not only the students who actively answer the questions but also the other students in the class who listen to the exchange of questions and responses.

## SELF-QUESTIONING: A TOOL FOR LEARNERS

Students may benefit from self-questioning as a metacognitive skill for learning. In an experimental study, researchers found that "metacognitive training in self-questioning enhances self-regulation and learning."[8] Students who think metacognitively often ask themselves internal questions that help them to analyze tasks. "What do I have to do? What are my options and strategies? How well did my choices work? What might I keep or change for next time?"[9] Music teachers can aid students with task analysis by playing audio or video recordings of excellent work by previous students or by facilitating students' attendance at live performances by student musicians from other schools. Listening experiences such as these allow music learners to formulate concepts about the musical tasks set before them and to develop awareness of their own relative strengths and weaknesses.

Self-questioning is a natural part of learners' self-awareness, monitoring, and self-evaluation processes as they work through music-learning tasks. It is advantageous in many music-learning situations but may be detrimental to music performance. In their book *The Inner Game of Music*, Green and Gallwey warn against allowing self-questioning to interfere with music performance. They refer to the internal voice that raises self-doubt during performance as *Self 1* and the productive, natural part of the musician as *Self 2*.[10]

> Self 1 is our interference. It contains our concepts about how things should be, our judgments and associations. It is particularly fond of the words *should* and *shouldn't* and often sees things in terms of what "could have been."
>
> Self 2 is the vast reservoir of potential within each one of us. It contains our natural talents and abilities and is a virtually unlimited resource that we can tap and develop. Left to its own devices, it performs with gracefulness and ease.[11]

When it comes to the usefulness of self-questioning in music learning, perhaps the matter of appropriate timing is most important. Music teachers will want to encourage students to use self-questioning as a tool for learning while they are engaged in problem-solving and decision-making phases of music learning and practice. Once students have mastered automatized motor responses for fluent performance of specific pieces in their repertoires, the act of self-questioning might get in the way of smooth, expressive, and rewarding performance experiences. When students begin to work on new pieces, they might once again use self-questioning for a new cycle of self-awareness, self-monitoring, and self-evaluation as they learn and practice the new repertoire.

## TEACHING PRODUCTIVE PRACTICE HABITS

Music teachers train their students to focus on self-regulatory habits as a way to help the students take responsibility for their own achievement.[12] For music learners to develop metacognitive self-regulation during independent practice, they must have a content-knowledge base and an aural-knowledge base. Beginning students will have neither. As students make progress in their music studies, they acquire both content knowledge and aural knowledge. For this reason, listening to appropriate musical models is important. Teachers might facilitate music learners' engaging in frequent, meaningful listening activities so that they can develop what Hallam called the "aural schemata required to develop an aural-knowledge base."[13] In this way, music learners can come to identify what the desirable outcomes from their practicing should be. As students develop expertise, teachers can expect them to listen to a broader range of repertoire and to engage in more complex metacognitive awareness of their own strengths and weaknesses.[14]

Hallam suggested that teachers can demonstrate productive practice habits. As students gain music knowledge and skills, "teachers can begin to demonstrate some of the processes underlying effective practice—for example, obtaining an overview of the work, identifying difficulties, selecting appropriate strategies, working on sections, integrating them into a whole, monitoring progress, setting goals, and evaluating." With developing expertise, teachers can encourage students to attend to "issues concerned with supporting learning, motivation, concentration, the organization and planning of practice, and developing strategies for ensuring optimum performance."[15]

Although teacher demonstration is invaluable, it is through independent practice that music learners acquire beneficial self-regulatory skills. Students will not develop self-regulation unless they are put in independent situations where they are free to make their own choices and control their own learning.[16] Teachers can direct every step of their students' work. In doing so, they might be modeling excellent metacognitive strategies. But if the students have no control over their own learning, they will not learn to think metacognitively on their own. Conversely, teachers cannot leave the development of metacognition to chance, either. After modeling effective learning strategies, teachers can ask students to choose from among several options for completing a learning task. Subsequently, teachers can ask students to assess which strategies worked best for them and why. In this way, there is a balance between teacher dominance of the learning process and complete student self-direction. A balanced approach is likely to lead students toward self-regulation of their learning processes.[17]

## INVITING METACOGNITIVE DIALOGUE

Teachers help learners build metacognitive skills when they invite them to share in planning, monitoring, and evaluating their work. The following is a list of suggestions for incorporating metacognitive dialogue into music-learning situations.

- Music teachers can engage students in a brief "class meeting" at the beginning of a music class or rehearsal in which students have input into setting goals for the class. At the end of the class or rehearsal, the teacher can invite students to share their reflections and evaluations regarding the success of the class or rehearsal.[18]
- *Prior* to a learning activity, music teachers can invite students to set goals and map out some step-by-step plans to achieve their goals. *During* a learning activity, teachers can ask students to share their progress. *After* a learning activity, teachers can invite students to decide whether they followed their plans as expected and whether

they achieved their goals. Additionally, teachers might ask students to speculate as to whether they should have used different strategies and whether they will set different goals or make different plans in the future.[19]

- Music teachers can help students to build metacognitive skills by imagining what the thinking skills of famous composers or performers might be. In a class discussion, teachers might lead students to speculate on the mental powers of others as a way to grasp the idea of thinking about thinking. What were the thought processes that led Mozart, Beethoven, or other great composers to create music that has lived on through the centuries? What are the thought processes of great contemporary artists that allow them to present memorable performances, inspiring awe in their audiences? When students are invited to share their answers to these questions, they might begin to consider how thought processes operate in music making.[20]

Music teachers can invite students to explain processes that take place in day-to-day classes and rehearsals. In so doing, students will need to think metacognitively. Some strategies include the following:

- Invite students to participate in setting musical goals for themselves and their performing ensembles.
- Invite students to share their perceptions about musical tasks—difficulties, potential problem spots, corrections, opportunities for expression, or feelings of accomplishment.
- Invite students to analyze music-learning tasks and select the strategies and skills that they think are most appropriate to completing the tasks.

---

**Tips for Teachers**

Do you sometimes feel that you are in a teaching rut, saying and doing the same things over and over? To alleviate that burned-out feeling, try using metacognitive skills in your own professional tasks. Additionally, try planning and implementing instruction that solicits metacognition from your students. You will benefit from injecting an emphasis on higher-level-thinking skills into your teaching and your daily professional activities.

- Invite students to participate in planning for learning—repertoire selection, rehearsal procedures, concert preparations, and group motivation.
- Invite students to explain how specific music-learning experiences affect them as musicians—performances, contests, composition projects, improvisatory experiences, or listening experiences.
- Invite students to model music-skill-learning strategies for other students.

## TEACHER MODELING

Teacher modeling has the greatest influence on students developing metacognitive skills.[21] When teachers model metacognitive skills for problem solving, they can explain their processes sequentially, including (1) setting goals, (2) selecting and applying procedures, (3) specifying rules to be followed, and (4) describing potential obstacles that might occur. While modeling metacognitive processes, teachers can explain their decisions as they work through a problem, and they can share their reflective self-evaluations at the end of a demonstration.[22] Teachers can let students know that, although the teacher might not have an immediate answer to every question, he or she can devise strategies to finding correct answers. Similarly, teachers can demonstrate to students that, although the teacher sometimes makes mistakes, he or she does know how to get back on track. In so doing, teachers need not fear demonstrating their own strengths and weaknesses for their students. It is valuable for students to see how experts are able to build on their strengths and apply strategies to overcome weaknesses.[23]

In chapter 6 of this book, think-aloud protocol was presented as a way for students to share metacognitive information with fellow students while working through music-learning tasks. The act of thinking aloud is also an effective way for teachers to model metacognitive skills for their students. Teachers might verbalize their own thoughts as they work through music-learning problems to show students how a skilled thinker approaches the tasks.[24]

The idea of modeling metacognitive skills might be more crucial for music teachers than for teachers in academic subject areas because of the nature of music teaching as performing. Richard Kennell pointed out this paradox when he noted that "when music teachers teach, they simultaneously perform. We make music with our students. I cannot think of another subject area in which the roles of teacher and student are so intertwined. Our music making is a joint activity that combines the responsibilities and actions of the teacher with the responsibilities and actions of our students."[25]

Because of this relationship between music teacher and students, a situation develops in which much of the work of the music teacher (especially an ensemble director) takes place out of sight of the students. Repertoire selection, score study, focused listening, and analytical planning for desired musical outcomes all occur before the teacher steps in front of the class or onto the conductor's podium. Rehearsal procedures and conducting gestures proceed from the director in a seemingly effortless manner. Students do not realize that automatic and effective behaviors of the director are the result of years of conscious training. Directors who want to model metacognition for their students will need to make a concerted effort to share with them some of the decision-making processes that precede a smooth and effective rehearsal. Shared information might include the rationale for repertoire selection, concepts formulated from score study, and ideas

**Photo 8.2. High School Band, Low Brass**

conceived during focused listening to recorded models. Kennell believes that "the music teacher should always be a model for successful music-thinking skills."[26]

## TEACHERS' PERSONAL METACOGNITION

Because they make thousands of moment-by-moment decisions every day, teachers must monitor and control their own thought processes while they are teaching. As teachers gain experience, they use reflection and self-regulation to find instructional strategies that work in the classroom and thereby develop teaching expertise.[27] Teachers can use metacognition to think about their own teaching, reflecting on their instructional goals, instructional strategies, and assessment of student achievement. Metacognition allows teachers to exert awareness and control over how they are teaching. Consequently, teachers can self-regulate as they plan, monitor, and evaluate their own teaching procedures and outcomes, engaging in these metacognitive activities before, during, and after teaching lessons or conducting rehearsals.[28]

Teachers need to have declarative, procedural, and conditional metacognitive knowledge about their own teaching. Declarative knowledge helps to answer questions like *What do I do when I am teaching?* Procedural knowledge helps teachers know how to go about the tasks of teaching specific content and skills so that students achieve desired learning outcomes. Conditional knowledge allows teachers to know when and why to apply specific instructional strategies.

Hope Hartman asserted that "teachers need to have a repertoire of teaching strategies to allow them to be flexible and shift as the situation requires. Even the most effective instructional technique does not work in all situations, and variety is necessary to prevent boredom. Strategic metacognitive knowledge about teaching strategies can help teachers compare various methods that might be used to achieve the same academic objectives and evaluate the advantages and disadvantages of each."[29] Studies of expert teachers suggest a high level of metacognitive thinking. Expert teachers demonstrate ability to make decisions in response to unpredictable situations in the classroom and appear to know what actions will be successful and why.[30]

Similarly, it is important for teachers to possess metacognitive knowledge of thinking skills so that they can transfer awareness of their own metacognition into approaches for teaching their students. It is through such awareness that teachers can (1) introduce metacognitive activities in class, (2) design high-quality learning experiences for students, and (3) teach higher-order thinking skills in their classrooms.[31] Interestingly, Duffy, Miller, Parsons, and Meloth reported that researchers found greater use of metacognition among teachers when they involved students in challenging tasks that require higher-order thinking skills. Conversely, when teachers involved students in closed tasks, such as worksheets, the teachers did not use metacognition to such a great extent. These results led researchers to conclude that the level of metacognitive skill employed by teachers might be tied to the types of tasks that they assign to their students.[32]

Thinking about thinking can benefit teachers as professional practitioners and students as learners. Assignments, procedures, activities, and behaviors that require students to think about thinking can be embedded in content instruction, rehearsals, creative projects, and independent practice. Metacognition can enrich the myriad of learning tasks associated with music education and thereby increase learning opportunities for students.


## NOTES

1. Nancy Joseph, "Metacognition Needed: Teaching Middle and High School Students to Develop Strategic Learning Skills," *Preventing School Failure* 54, no. 2 (2010): 100.

2. Susan Hallam, "The Development of Metacognition in Musicians: Implications for Education," *British Journal of Music Education* 4, no. 1 (2001): 38.

3. Arthur L. Costa and Lawrence F. Lowery, *Techniques for Teaching Thinking* (Pacific Grove, Calif.: Midwest Publications, 1989), 22–23.

4. Ibid., 34.

5. Ibid., 41.

6. Ibid., 42.

7. Ibid. 44–45.

8. Valentina McInerney and Dennis M. McInerney, "Metacognitive Strategy Training in Self-Questioning: The Strengths of Multimethod Investigations

of the Comparative Effects of Two Instructional Approaches on Self-Efficacy and Achievement" (paper presented at the annual meeting of the American Education Research Association, San Diego, Calif., April 13–17, 1998), 4.

9. Graham Foster, Evelyn Sawicki, Hyacinth Schaeffer, and Victor Zelinski, *I Think, Therefore I Learn!* (Markham, Ontario, Canada: Pembroke Publishers, 2002), 5.

10. Barry Green and W. Timothy Gallwey, *The Inner Game of Music* (New York: Doubleday, 1986), 16.

11. Ibid.

12. Siw G. Nielsen, "Self-Regulating Learning Strategies in Instrumental Music Practice," *Music Education Research* 3, no. 2 (2001): 166.

13. Susan Hallam, "Approaches to Instrumental Music Practice of Experts and Novices: Implications for Education," in *Does Practice Make Perfect? Current Theory and Research on Instrumental Music Practice*, edited by Harald Jørgensen and Andreas Lehmann (Oslo: Norges Musikkhøgskole, 1997), 104.

14. Ibid., 105.

15. Ibid., 104–105.

16. Nielsen, "Self-Regulating Learning Strategies," 166.

17. Foster, Sawicki, Shaeffer, and Zelinski, *I Think*, 11.

18. Costa and Lowery, "Techniques," 68.

19. Arthur L. Costa, "Mediating the Metacognitive," *Educational Leadership* 42 (1984): 59.

20. Ibid., 72.

21. Ibid.

22. Barry K. Beyer, *Practical Strategies for the Teaching of Thinking* (Boston: Allyn and Bacon, 1987), 200.

23. Costa and Lowery, "Techniques," 73.

24. Joseph, "Metacognition Needed," 101.

25. Richard Kennell, "Musical Thinking in the Instrumental Rehearsal," in *Dimensions of Musical Thinking*, edited by Eunice Boardman (Reston, Va.: MENC, 2002), 189.

26. Ibid., 194.

27. Gerald G. Duffy, Samuel Miller, Seth Parsons, and Michael Meloth, "Teachers as Metacognitive Professionals," in *Handbook of Metacognition in Education*, edited by Douglas J. Hacker, John Dunlosky, and Arthur C. Graesser (New York: Routledge, 2009), 241–42.

28. Hope J. Hartman, "Teaching Metacognitively," in *Metacognition in Learning and Instruction: Theory, Research and Practice*, edited by Hope J. Hartman (Dordrecht, Netherlands: Kluwer Academic Publishers, 2001), 150–52.

29. Ibid., 161–62.

30. Duffy, Miller, Parsons, and Meloth, "Teachers as Metacognitive Professionals," 245–46.

31. Anat Zohar, "Teachers' Metacognitive Knowledge and the Instruction of Higher Order Thinking," *Teaching and Teacher Education* 15 (1999): 418.

32. Duffy, Miller, Parsons, and Meloth, "Teachers as Metacognitive Professionals," 246.

# BIBLIOGRAPHY

Aitchison, Randall E. "The Effects of Self-Evaluation Techniques on the Musical Performance, Self-Evaluation Accuracy, Motivation, and Self-Esteem of Middle School Instrumental Music Students." Ph.D. diss., University of Iowa, ProQuest UMI Dissertations Publishing, 1995. 304196547.

Anderson, Lorin W., David R. Krathwohl, Peter W. Airasian, Kathleen A. Cruikshank, Richard E. Mayer, Paul R. Pintrich, James Raths, and Merlin C. Wittrock. *A Taxonomy for Learning, Teaching, and Assessing: A Revision of Bloom's Taxonomy of Education Objectives*. New York: Longman, 2001.

Bach, Johann Sebastian. *Ach Gott und Herr, wie Gross und Schwer*, BWV 255. Edited by Claudio Macchi. http://www1.cpdl.org/wiki/images/9/99/Bwv-ach1.pdf (accessed May 27, 2013).

———. *Alle Menschen Müssen Sterben*, BWV 262. Edited by Claudio Macchi. http://www0.cpdl.org/wiki/images/7/7e/Bwv-allm.pdf (accessed May 27, 2013).

Barell, John. *Teaching for Thoughtfulness: Classroom Strategies to Enhance Intellectual Development*. White Plains, N.Y.: Longman Publishing Group, 1991.

Barell, John, Rosemarie Liebmann, and Irving Sigel. "Fostering Thoughtful Self-Direction in Students." *Educational Leadership* 45, no. 7 (1988): 14–17.

Barry, Nancy H. "The Effects of Practice Strategies, Individual Differences in Cognitive Style, and Gender upon Technical Accuracy and Musicality of Student Instrumental Performance." *Psychology of Music* 20 (1992): 112–23.

Barry, Nancy H., and Susan Hallam. "Practice." In *The Science and Psychology of Music Performance*, edited by Richard Parncutt and Gary E. McPherson, 151–65. New York: Oxford University Press, 2002.

Barry, Nancy H., and Victoria McArthur. "Teaching Practice Strategies in the Music Studio: A Survey of Applied Music Teachers." *Psychology of Music* 22 (1994): 44–55.

Bathgate, Meghan, Judith Sims-Knight, and Christian Schunn. "Thoughts on Thinking: Engaging Novice Music Students in Metacognition." *Applied Cognitive Psychology* 26, no. 2 (2012): 403–409. doi:10.1002/acp.1842.

Bauer, William I. "Metacognition and Middle School Band Students," *Journal of Band Research* 43, no. 2 (2008): 50–63.

Benton, Carol. "A Study of the Effects of Metacognition on Student Learning Outcomes among Students in College Music Theory Classes." Paper presented at the College Music Society Southern Chapter Regional Conference, Tampa, Fla., February 24, 2012.

———. "But, What Will They Think? Strategies for Promoting Metacognition among Students in Music Classes and Performing Ensembles." Interest session, Georgia Music Educators Association In-Service Conference, Savannah, Ga., January 2011.

Bereiter, Carl, and Marlene Scardamalia. "Cognition and Curriculum." In *Handbook of Research on Curriculum: A Project of the American Educational Research Association*, edited by Philip W. Jackson, 517–37. New York: MacMillan, 1992.

Berg, Margaret H. "Getting the Minutes In: A Case Study of Beginning Instrumentalists' Music Practice." In *Diverse Methodologies in the Study of Music Teaching and Learning*, edited by Linda K. Thompson and Mark Robin Campbell, 45–65. Charlotte, N.C.: Information Age Publishing, 2008.

Bergee, Martin J. "A Comparison of Faculty, Peer, and Self-Evaluation of Applied Brass Jury Performances." *Journal of Research in Music Education* 41, no. 1 (1993): 19–27.

Bergee, Martin J., and Lecia Cecconi-Roberts. "Effects of Small-Group Peer Interaction on Self-Evaluation of Music Performance." *Journal of Research in Music Education* 50, no. 3 (2002): 256–68.

Beyer, Barry K. *Practical Strategies for the Teaching of Thinking*. Boston: Allyn and Bacon, 1987.

Biggs, John. "Student Approaches to Learning." http://www.johnbiggs.com.au/academic/students-approaches-to-learning/ (accessed December 18, 2013).

Biggs, John, David Kember, and Doris Y. P. Leung. "The Revised Two Factor Study Process Questionnaire: R-SPQ-2F." *British Journal of Educational Psychology* 71 (2001): 136–37.

Boardman, Eunice. "The Relationship of Musical Thinking and Learning to Classroom Instruction." In *Dimensions of Musical Learning and Teaching: A Different Kind of Classroom*, edited by Eunice Boardman, 1–20. Reston, Va.: MENC, 2002.

Brown, Ann. "Knowing When, Where, and How to Remember: A Problem of Metacognition." In *Advances in Instructional Psychology, volume 1*, edited by Robert Glaser, 77–165. Hillsdale, N.J.: Lawrence Erlbaum Associates, 1978.

Byo, James L., and Jane W. Cassidy. "An Exploratory Study of Time Use in the Practice of Music Majors: Self-Report and Observation Analysis." *Update: Applications of Research in Music Education* 27, no. 1. (2008): 33–40.

Cantwell, Robert H., and Yvette Millard. "The Relationship between Approach to Learning and Learning Strategies in Learning Music." *British Journal of Educational Psychology* 64, no. 1 (1994): 45–63.

Chiu, Ming Ming, and Sze Wing Kuo. "Social Metacognition in Groups: Benefits, Difficulties, Learning, and Teaching." In *Metacognition: New Research Developments*, edited by Clayton B. Larson, 117–36. New York: Nova Science Publishers, 2009.

Cobb, Paul, Ada Boufi, Kay McClain, and Joy Whitenack. "Reflective Discourse and Collective Reflection." *Journal for Research in Mathematics Education* 28, no. 3 (1997): 258–77.

Colwell, Richard. "Roles of Direct Instruction, Critical Thinking, and Transfer in the Design of Curriculum for Music Learning." In *MENC Handbook of Research on Music Learning: vol. 1, Strategies*, edited by Richard Colwell and Peter R. Webster, 84–139. New York: Oxford University Press, 2011.

Costa, Arthur L., "Mediating the Metacognitive." *Educational Leadership* 42 (1984): 57–62.

Costa, Arthur L., and Lawrence F. Lowery. *Techniques for Teaching Thinking*. Pacific Grove, Calif.: Midwest Publications, 1989.

Cunningham, Judy, Carol Krull, Nora Land, and Sylvia Russell. "Motivating Students to be Self-Reflective Learners through Goal-Setting and Self-Evaluation." Action Research Project, Saint Xavier University and Skylight Professional Development, 2000.

Daniel, Ryan. "Self-Assessment in Performance." *British Journal of Music Education* 18, no. 3 (2001): 215–26.

Davidson, Janet E., and Robert J. Sternberg. "Smart Problem Solving: How Metacognition Helps." In *Metacognition in Educational Theory and Practice*, edited by Douglas J. Hacker, John Dunlosky, and Arthur Graesser, 47–68. Mahwah, N.J.: Lawrence Erlbaum Associates, 1998.

Davidson, Lyle, and Larry Scripp. "Education and Development in Music from a Cognitive Perspective." In *Children and the Arts*, edited by David J. Hargreaves, 58–86. Philadelphia: Open University Press, 1989.

———. "Tracing Reflective Thinking in the Performance Ensemble." *Quarterly Journal of Music Teaching and Learning* 1, no. 1 (1990): 49–62.

Dawson, Peg, and Richard Guare. *Smart but Scattered: The Revolutionary "Executive Skills" Approach to Helping Kids Reach Their Potential*. New York: The Guilford Press, 2009.

Desautel, Daric. "Becoming a Thinking Thinker: Metacognition, Self-Reflection, and Classroom Practice." *Teachers College Record* 111, no. 8 (2009): 1997–2020.

Dewey, John. *How We Think: A Restatement of the Relation of Reflective Thinking to the Educative Process*. New York: D. C. Heath and Company, 1933.

Dobbs, Teryl L. "Discourse in the Band Room: The Role of Talk in an Instrumental Music Classroom." In *Diverse Methodologies in the Study of Music Teaching and Learning*, edited by Linda K. Thompson and Mark Robin Campbell, 137–62. Charlotte, N.C.: Information Age Publishing, 2008.

Duffy, Gerald G., Samuel Miller, Seth Parsons, and Michael Meloth. "Teachers as Metacognitive Professionals." In *Handbook of Metacognition in Education*, edited by Douglas J. Hacker, John Dunlosky, and Arthur C. Graesser, 240–56. New York: Routledge, 2009.

Duke, Robert A., Amy L. Simmons, and Carla D. Cash. "It's Not How Much; It's How." *Journal of Research in Music Education* 56, no. 4 (2009): 310–21.

Dunlosky, John, and Janet Metcalfe. *Metacognition*. Thousand Oaks, Calif.: SAGE Publications, 2009.

Egan, Marilyn M. "Effects of Metacognition on Music Achievement of University Students." Ph.D. diss., Kent State University, ProQuest, UMI Dissertations Publishing, 1995. 9536648.

Everson, Howard T., Sigmund Tobias, and Vytas Laitusis. "Do Metacognitive Skills and Learning Strategies Transfer across Domains?" Paper presented at the Annual Meeting of the American Educational Research Association, Chicago, Ill., March 24–28, 1997.

Farrell, Susan. *Tools for Powerful Student Evaluation*. Ft. Lauderdale, Fla.: Meredith Music Publications, 1997.

Flavell, John H. "Metacognition and Cognitive Monitoring: A New Area of Cognitive Developmental Inquiry." *American Psychologist* 34, no. 10 (1979): 906–11.

———. "Metacognitive Aspects of Problem Solving." In *The Nature of Intelligence*, edited by Lauren B. Resnick, 231–36. Hillsdale, N.J.: Lawrence Erlbaum Associates, 1976.

Foster, Graham, Evelyn Sawicki, Hyacinth Shaeffer, and Victor Zelinski. *I Think, Therefore I Learn!* Markham, Ontario, Canada: Pembroke Publishers, 2002.

Fox, Emily, and Michelle Riconscente. "Metacognition and Self-Regulation in James, Piaget, and Vygotsky." *Educational Psychology Review* 20, no. 4 (2008): 373–89.

Gagné, Robert M., and Mary Perkins Driscoll. *Essentials of Learning for Instruction*. Englewood Cliffs, N.J.: Prentice-Hall, 1988.

Georghiades, Petros. "From the General to the Situated: Three Decades of Metacognition." *International Journal of Science Education* 26, no. 3 (2004): 365–83.

Georgia Music Educators Association. "Choral Large Group Adjudication Form." http://opus.gmea.org/Pages/Forum/ViewForum.aspx?Forum=5 (accessed July 8, 2012).

Goldberg, Pat. *Increasing Problem Solving through the Metacognitive Skills of Planning, Monitoring, and Evaluating*. Eric Document ED 439 160. Chicago: Spencer Foundation, 1999.

Green, Barry, and W. Timothy Gallwey. *The Inner Game of Music*. New York: Doubleday, 1986.

Gruson, Linda M. "Rehearsal Skill and Musical Competence: Does Practice Make Perfect?" In *Generative Processes in Music: The Psychology of Performance, Improvisation, and Composition*, edited by John A. Sloboda, 91–112. New York: Oxford University Press, 1988.

Hacker, Douglas J. "Definitions and Empirical Foundations." In *Metacognition in Educational Theory and Practice*, edited by Douglas J. Hacker, John Dunlosky, and Arthur C. Graesser, 1–23. Mahwah, N.J.: Lawrence Erlbaum Associates, 1998.

Hale, Connie L., and Susan K. Green. "Six Key Principles for Music Assessment." *Music Educators Journal* 95, no. 4 (2009): 27–33.

Hallam, Susan. "Approaches to Instrumental Music Practice of Experts and Novices: Implications for Education." In *Does Practice Make Perfect? Current Theory and Research on Instrumental Music Practice*, edited by Harald Jørgensen and Andreas Lehmann, 89–107. Oslo: Norges Musikkhøgskole, 1997.

———. "The Development of Expertise in Young Musicians: Strategy Use, Knowledge Acquisition and Individual Diversity." *Music Education Research* 3, no.1 (2001): 7–23.

———. "The Development of Metacognition in Musicians: Implications for Education." *British Journal of Music Education* 4, no. 1 (2001): 27–39.

———. "What Do We Know about Practicing? Towards a Model Synthesising the Research Literature." In *Does Practice Make Perfect? Current Theory and Research on Instrumental Music Practice*, edited by Harald Jørgensen and Andreas Lehmann, 179–231. Oslo: Norges Musikkhøgskole, 1997.

Halpern, Diane F. "Teaching Critical Thinking for Transfer across Domains: Dispositions, Skills, Structure Training, and Metacognitive Monitoring." *American Psychologist* 53, no. 4 (1998): 449–54.

Hanna, Wendell. "The New Bloom's Taxonomy: Implications for Music Education." *Arts Education Policy Review* 108, no. 4 (2007): 7–16.

Hartman, Hope J. "Developing Students' Metacognitive Knowledge and Skills." In *Metacognition in Learning and Instruction: Theory, Research and Practice*, edited by Hope J. Hartman, 33–68. Dordrecht, Netherlands: Kluwer Academic Publishers, 2001.

———. "Teaching Metacognitively." In *Metacognition in Learning and Instruction: Theory, Research and Practice*, edited by Hope J. Hartman, 149–72. Dordrecht, Netherlands: Kluwer Academic Publishers, 2001.

Hewitt, Michael P. "The Effects of Modeling, Self-Evaluation, and Self-Listening on Junior High Instrumentalists' Music Performance and Practice Attitude." *Journal of Research in Music Education* 49, no. 4 (2001): 307–22.

———. "The Impact of Self-Evaluation Instruction on Student Self-Evaluation, Music Performance, and Self-Evaluation Accuracy." *Journal of Research in Music Education* 59, no. 1 (2011): 6–20.

———. "Self-Evaluation Accuracy among High School and Middle School Instrumentalists." *Journal of Research in Music Education* 53, no. 2 (2005): 148–61.

———. "Self-Evaluation Tendencies of Junior High Instrumentalists." *Journal of Research in Music Education* 50, no. 3 (2002): 215–26.

Hirsch, E. D., Jr. *The Schools We Need and Why We Don't Have Them*. New York: Doubleday, 1996.

Homan, Annaliese. *Constructing Knowledge through Reflection*. Phoenix: League for Innovation in the Community College, 2006.

Jager, de Bernadette, Margo Jansen, and Gerry Reezigt. "The Development of Metacognition in Primary School Learning Environments." *School Effectiveness and School Improvement* 16, no. 2 (2005): 179–96.

Johnson, Daniel. "The Effect of Critical Thinking Instruction on Verbal Descriptions of Music." *Journal of Research in Music Education* 59, no. 3 (2011): 257–72.

Joseph, Nancy. "Metacognition Needed: Teaching Middle and High School Students to Develop Strategic Learning Skills." *Preventing School Failure* 54, no. 2 (2010): 99–103.

Kennell, Richard. "Musical Thinking in the Instrumental Rehearsal." In *Dimensions of Musical Thinking*, edited by Eunice Boardman, 187–97. Reston, Va.: MENC, 2002.

Kerka, Sandra. "Journal Writing as an Adult Learning Tool: Practice Application Brief No. 22." Sponsored by the Office of Educational Research and Improvement (ED). Columbus, Ohio: ERIC Clearing House on Adult, Career, and Vocational Education, 2002. http://files.eric.ed.gov/fulltext/ED470782.pdf.

Kincannon, Joyce, Conrad Gleber, and Jaehyun Kim. "The Effects of Metacognitive Training on Performance and Use of Metacognitive Skills in Self-Directed Learning Situations." Paper presented at the National Convention of the Association for Educational Communications and Technology, Houston, Tex., 1999.

Kohut, Daniel. *Musical Performance: Learning Theory and Pedagogy.* Englewood Cliffs, N.J.: Prentice-Hall, 1985.

Kostka, Marilyn J. "Effects of Self-Assessment and Successive Approximations on 'Knowing' and 'Valuing' Selected Keyboard Skills." *Journal of Research in Music Education* 45, no. 2 (1997): 273–81.

Kuhn, Deanna. "A Developmental Model of Critical Thinking." *Educational Researcher* 28, no. 2 (1999): 16–25, 46.

Lehmann, Andreas C., and Jane W. Davidson. "Taking an Acquired Skills Perspective on Music Performance." In *MENC Handbook of Musical Cognition and Development*, edited by Richard Colwell, 225–58. New York: Oxford University Press, 2006.

Lehmann, Andreas C., and K. Anders Ericsson. "Research on Expert Performance and Deliberate Practice: Implications for the Education of Amateur Musicians and Music Students." *Psychomusicology* 16, no. 1–2 (1997): 40–58.

Leon-Guerrero, Amanda. "Self-Regulation Strategies Used by Student Musicians during Music Practice." *Music Education Research* 10, no. 1 (2008): 91–106.

Lisk, Edward. *The Creative Director: Conductor, Teacher, Leader.* Galesville, Md.: Meredith Music Publications, 2006. Kindle edition.

Lochhead, Jack. "Sound Thinking with Thinkback 2000." Paper presented at the Technological Education and National Development Conference, "Crossroads of the Millennium," April 8–10, 2000, Abu Dhabi, United Arab Emirates.

Martinez, Michael E. "What Is Metacognition?" *Phi Delta Kappan* 87, no. 9 (2006): 696–99.

Marzano, Robert J. *A Different Kind of Classroom: Teaching with Dimensions of Learning.* Alexandria, Va.: Association for Supervision and Curriculum Development, 1992.

Marzano, Robert J., and John S. Kendall. *Designing and Assessing Education Objectives: Applying the New Taxonomy.* Thousand Oaks, Calif.: Corwin Press, 2008.

———. *The New Taxonomy of Educational Objectives.* Thousand Oaks, Calif.: Corwin Press, 2007.

Masui, Chris, and Erik DeCorte. "Enhancing Learning and Problem Solving Skills: Orienting and Self-Judging, Two Powerful and Trainable Learning Tools." *Learning and Instruction* 9 (1999): 517–42.

Mathias, Sandra L. "A Teaching Technique to Aid the Development of Vocal Accuracy in Elementary School Students." Ph.D. diss., Ohio State University, UMI Dissertations Publishing, 1997. 9735675.

May, Lissa F. "Factors and Abilities Influencing Achievement in Instrumental Jazz Improvisation." *Journal of Research in Music Education* 51, no. 3 (2003): 245–58.

McInerney, Valentina, and Dennis M. McInerney. "Metacognitive Strategy Training in Self-Questioning: The Strengths of Multimethod Investigations of the Comparative Effects of Two Instructional Approaches on Self-Efficacy and Achievement." Paper presented at the Annual Meeting of the American Education Research Association, San Diego, Calif., April 13–17, 1998.

McNamara, Danielle S., and Joseph P. Magliano. "The Dynamics of Reading." In *Handbook of Metacognition in Education*, edited by Douglas J. Hacker, John Dunlosky, and Arthur C. Graesser, 60–82. New York: Routledge, 2009.

McPhail, Graham J. "Crossing Boundaries: Sharing Concepts of Music Teaching from Classroom to Studio." *Music Education Research* 12, no. 1 (2010): 33–45.

McPherson, Gary E. "Cognitive Strategies and Skill Acquisition in Musical Performance." *Bulletin of the Council for Research in Music Education*, no. 133 (Summer 1997): 64–71.

McPherson, Gary E., and Barry J. Zimmerman. "Self-Regulation of Musical Learning: A Social Cognitive Perspective on Developing Performance Skills." In *MENC Handbook of Research on Music Learning, vol. 2: Applications*, edited by Richard Colwell and Peter R. Webster, 130–75. New York: Oxford University Press, 2011.

McPherson, Gary E., and James M. Renwick. "A Longitudinal Study of Self-Regulation in Children's Musical Practice." *Music Education Research* 3, no. 2 (2001): 169–86.

McPherson, Gary E., and John McCormick. "Motivational and Self-Regulated Learning Components of Musical Practice." *Bulletin of the Council for Research in Music Education*, no. 141 (Summer 1999): 98–102.

MENC. "National Music Adjudication Coalition Concert Band or Orchestra Music Assessment Form." http://musiced.nafme.org/files/2013/02/NMACbandorchestraform.pdf (accessed December 17, 2013).

Metcalfe, Janet, and Hedy Kober. "Self-Reflective Consciousness and the Projectable Self." In *The Missing Link in Cognition: Origins of Self-Reflective Consciousness*, edited by Herbert S. Terrace and Janet Metcalfe, 57–83. New York: Oxford University Press, 2005.

Miklaszewski, Kacper. "A Case Study of a Pianist Preparing a Musical Performance." *Psychology of Music* 17, no. 2 (1989): 95–109.

Miksza, Peter. "The Development of a Measure of Self-Regulated Practice Behavior for Beginning and Intermediate Instrumental Music Students." *Journal of Research in Music Education* 59, no. 4 (2012): 319–38.

———. "Relationships among Impulsiveness, Locus of Control, Sex, and Music Practice." *Journal of Research in Music Education* 54, no. 4 (2006): 308–23.

Miksza, Peter, Stephanie Prichard, and Diana Sorbo. "An Observational Study of Intermediate Band Students' Self-Regulated Practice Behaviors." *Journal of Research in Music Education* 60, no. 3 (2012): 254–66.

Morrison, Steven J., Mark Montemayor, and Eric S. Wiltshire. "The Effect of a Recorded Model on Band Students' Performance Self-Evaluations, Achievement and Attitude." *Journal of Research in Music Education* 52, no. 2 (2004): 116–129.

National Association for Music Education. "National Standards for Music Education." http://musiced.nafme.org/resources/national-standards-for-music-education/ (accessed August 4, 2013).

Nelson, Darolyne L. "High-Risk Adolescent Males, Self-Efficacy, and Choral Performance: An Investigation of Affective Intervention." DMA diss., Arizona State University, ProQuest, UMI Dissertations Publishing, 1997. 9725321.

Nielsen, Siw G. "Learning Strategies in Instrumental Music Practice." *British Journal of Music Education* 16, no. 3 (1999): 275–91.

———. "Self-Regulating Learning Strategies in Instrumental Music Practice." *Music Education Research* 3, no. 2 (2001): 155–67.

———. "Self-Regulation of Learning Strategies during Practice: A Case Study of a Church Organ Student Preparing a Musical Work for Performance." In *Does Practice Make Perfect? Current Theory and Research on Instrumental Music Practice*, edited by Harald Jørgensen and Andreas Lehmann, 109–22. Oslo: Norges Musikkhøgskole, 1997.

Oare, Steve. "Decisions Made in the Practice Room: A Qualitative Study of Middle School Students' Thought Processes while Practicing." *Update: Applications of Research in Music Education* 30, no. 2 (2012): 63–70.

Paris, Scott G., Marjorie Y. Lipson, and Karen K. Wixson. "Becoming a Strategic Reader." *Contemporary Educational Psychology* 8, no. 3 (1983): 293–316.

Perkins, D. N. *The Mind's Best Work*. Cambridge, Mass.: Harvard University Press, 1981.

Peters, Michael A. "Kinds of Thinking, Styles of Reasoning." In *Critical Thinking and Learning*, edited by Mark Mason, 12–24. Malden, Mass.: Blackwell Publishing, 2008.

Pitts, Stephanie, Jane Davidson, and Gary McPherson. "Developing Effective
    Practice Strategies: Case Studies of Three Young Instrumentalists." *Music
    Education Research* 2, no. 1 (2000): 45–56.
Pogonowski, Lenore. "Metacognition: A Dimension of Musical Thinking." In
    *Dimensions of Musical Thinking*, edited by Eunice Boardman, 9–19. Reston,
    Va.: MENC, 1989.
Presseisen, Barbara Z. *Thinking Skills: Research and Practice*. Washington,
    D.C.: National Education Association, 1986.
Reimer, Bennett. *A Philosophy of Music Education: Advancing the Vision*. Up-
    per Saddle River, N.J.: Pearson Education, 2003.
Richardson, Carol P., and Nancy L. Whitaker. "Critical Thinking and Music
    Education." In *Handbook of Research on Music Teaching and Learning*,
    edited by Richard Colwell, 546–57. New York: Schirmer Books, 1992.
Robinson, Nathalie G., Cindy L. Bell, and Lenore Pogonowski. "The Creative
    Music Strategy." *Music Educators Journal* 97, no. 3 (2011): 50–55.
Rohwer, Debbie, and Jeremy Polk. "Practice Behaviors of Eighth-Grade In-
    strumental Musicians." *Journal of Research in Music Education* 54, no. 4
    (2006): 350–62.
Schraw, Gregory. "Promoting General Metacognitive Awareness." *Instruc-
    tional Science* 26, no. 1–2 (1998): 113–25.
———. "Promoting General Metacognitive Awareness." In *Metacognition in
    Learning and Instruction: Theory, Research and Practice*, edited by Hope
    Hartman, 3–16. Dordrecht, Netherlands: Kluwer Academic Publishers,
    2001.
Schraw, Gregory, Kent J. Crippen, and Kendall Hartley. "Promoting Self-
    Regulation in Science Education: Metacognition as Part of a Broader Per-
    spective on Learning." *Research in Science Education* 36 (2006): 111–39.
Scott, Sheila. "A Constructivist View of Music Education: Perspectives for
    Deep Learning." *General Music Today* 19, no. 2 (2006): 17–21.
———. "A Minds-On Approach to Active Learning in General Music." *General
    Music Today* 24, no. 1 (2010): 19–26.
Sloboda, John A., Jane W. Davidson, Michael J. A. Howe, and Derek G. Moore.
    "The Role of Practice in the Development of Performing Musicians." *British
    Journal of Psychology* 87, no. 2 (1996): 287–309.
Swartz, Robert J., and D. N. Perkins. *Teaching Thinking: Issues and Ap-
    proaches*. Pacific Grove, Calif.: Midwest Publications, 1990.
Taylor, Shawn. "Better Learning through Better Thinking: Developing Stu-
    dents' Metacognitive Abilities." *Journal of College Reading and Learning* 30,
    no. 1 (1999): 34–45.
Tobias, Sigmund, Howard T. Everson, and Vytas Laitusis. "Towards a Perfor-
    mance Based Measure of Metacognitive Knowledge Monitoring: Relation-

ships with Self-Reports and Behavior Ratings." Paper presented at the Annual Meeting of the American Educational Research Association, Montreal, Quebec, Canada, April 1999.

Waters, Harriet S., and Thomas W. Kunnmann. "Metacognition and Strategy Discovery in Early Childhood." In *Metacognition, Strategy Use, and Instruction*, edited by Harriet S. Waters and Wolfgang Schneider, 3–22. New York: Guilford Press, 2009.

Weinstein, Claire E., and Richard E. Mayer. "The Teaching of Learning Strategies." *Innovation Abstracts* 5, no. 32 (1983). National Institute for Staff and Organizational Development.

Welsbacher, Betty T., and Elaine D. Bernstorf. "Musical Thinking among Diverse Students." In *Dimensions of Musical Learning and Teaching: A Different Kind of Classroom*, edited by Eunice Boardman, 155–67. Reston, Va.: MENC, 2002.

Whimbey, Arthur. "Students Can Learn to Be Better Problem Solvers." *Educational Leadership* 37, no. 7 (1980): 560–65.

Woody, Robert H. "Learning from the Experts: Applying Research in Expert Performance to Music Education." *Update: Applications of Research in Music Education* 19, no. 9 (2001): 9–14.

Zimmerman, Barry J. "Attaining Self-Regulation: A Social Cognitive Perspective." In *Handbook of Self-Regulation*, edited by Moske Zeidner, Paul R. Pintrich, and Monique Boekaerts, 13–39. San Diego: Academic Press, 2000.

Zimmerman, Barry J., and Adam R. Moylan. "Self-Regulation: Where Metacognition and Motivation Intersect." In *Handbook of Metacognition in Education*, edited by Douglas J. Hacker, John Dunlosky, and Arthur C. Graesser, 299–315. New York: Routledge, 2009.

Zohar, Anat. "Teachers' Metacognitive Knowledge and the Instruction of Higher Order Thinking." *Teaching and Teacher Education* 15 (1999): 413–29.

# ABOUT THE AUTHOR

**Carol Benton** holds a Bachelor of Music Education and Master of Music in piano performance from Virginia Commonwealth University, as well as a Doctor of Musical Arts in music education from Shenandoah Conservatory of Shenandoah University. After twenty-three years teaching choral and general music in Virginia public schools, Dr. Benton began teaching music-education courses on the college level. She has been on faculty at the University of Central Arkansas, Glenville State College (West Virginia), and Armstrong Atlantic State University (Georgia). Currently, Dr. Benton coordinates the BME degree program, teaches methods courses, and supervises music-education internships at Armstrong.